The New Twenty Years' Crisis

The New Twenty Years' Crisis

A Critique of International Relations, 1999–2019

PHILIP CUNLIFFE

McGill-Queen's University Press
Montreal & Kingston · London · Chicago

ISBN 978-0-2280-0101-0 (cloth)
ISBN 978-0-2280-0102-7 (paper)
ISBN 978-0-2280-0240-6 (ePDF)
ISBN 978-0-2280-0241-3 (ePUB)

Legal deposit third quarter 2020
Bibliothèque nationale du Québec

Printed in Canada on acid-free paper that is 100% ancient
forest free (100% post-consumer recycled), processed
chlorine free

We acknowledge the support of the Canada Council
for the Arts.

Nous remercions le Conseil des arts du Canada
de son soutien.

Library and Archives Canada Cataloguing in Publication

Title: The new twenty years' crisis : a critique of
   international relations, 1999–2019 / Philip Cunliffe.
Names: Cunliffe, Philip, author.
Description: Includes bibliographical references and index.
Identifiers: Canadiana (print) 20200213407 | Canadiana
   (ebook) 20200213415 | ISBN 9780228001010 (cloth) |
   ISBN 9780228001027 (paper) | ISBN 9780228002406
   (ePDF) | ISBN 9780228002413 (ePUB)
Subjects: LCSH: Carr, Edward Hallett, 1892–1982. Twenty
   years' crisis, 1919–1939. | LCSH: International relations—
   Philosophy. | LCSH: World politics—21st century. | LCSH:
   Liberalism. | LCSH: Utopia.
Classification: LCC JZ1305 .C86 2020 | DDC 327.101—dc23

Set in 9.5/13.5 Baskerville 10 Pro with Berthold Bodoni
Book design & typesetting by Garet Markvoort, zijn digital

For Mio

Contents

Preface and Acknowledgments ix

Introduction: Willing the End 3

1 Carr's Crisis and Ours, 1919–1939/1999–2019 32

2 Make IR Critical Again 60

3 Washed Up on the Shores of Eutopia 89

Conclusion: Beyond the Twenty Years' Crisis 118

Notes 129

Index 149

Preface and Acknowledgments

This book argues that we have been through a twenty years' crisis in which we have seen the degradation of liberal international order. We have now come through to the other side of that crisis, yet without being able to recognise our new political surroundings or identify the shape of a nascent new order. Instead, we remain ensnared in outmoded ideas, still unable to think politically as a result of inherited liberal dogma. This book seeks to reboot our thinking about international politics by critiquing prevailing ideas in International Relations (IR), the academic study of international politics.

I realised just how much my discipline of IR was in trouble, a few years back, while dawdling in an airport lounge en route from a major academic convention. I was chatting to a friend and colleague, also an IR academic, whose intellectual interests had, I felt, drifted in odd directions in recent years. It now dawned on me just how bad things had got when he told me that he was considering establishing a new journal, to be called "Critical Plant Studies." He was entirely confident that an array of academic publishers would support it, as there would definitely be a lucrative commercial demand for such a journal across the global university sector.

My colleague was only half-joking (I think). Joking or not, the most disturbing thing about this encounter was that I could myself easily see the intellectual rationale for such an endeavour. The table of contents, papers, conference proceedings and future intellectual twists and turns of this new discipline unfolded in my mind's eye deep into the future. For a start, root systems clearly represented a transgression against sovereign borders, as well as providing fresh, vegetal perspectives on transnational "movement" in an age of globalization. There were a few dozen workshops, special journal issues, and edited collections right there. These could be followed up with meta-analysis and critiques drawing on indigenous knowledges to contest patriarchal settler accounts of orthodox plant studies. Follow that up with the relational, non-essentialist ontologies that would be enabled by the (literal) hybridity of plant-based ways of life, and a whole new range of post-human insights could be used to disrupt the deeply-rooted preconceptions that underlie our anthropocentric distinctiveness and speciesist sexuality. I could even perceive the outline of a hitherto undreamt of intellectual challenge – one that went beyond anything as parochial as speciesism or as trivial as anthropocentrism (let alone Eurocentrism). For critical plant studies could subvert the exclusionary hegemony of the entire animal kingdom itself.[1]

Disturbed by these visions of rhizomatic revolt on my plane journey home, upon my return I rushed to Google and was immensely relieved to see that critical plant studies had in fact already put down roots as a new academic speciality over the last couple of years. Surely this meant that intellectual life in the academy could not rot any further. Yet my relief quickly gave way to doubt once again, as I noted that critical plant studies was planted, so to speak, at the intersection of philosophy, literature, and cultural studies. This inter-positional terrain would provide fertile soil for exactly the kind of trans-disciplinarity beloved by the bureaucrats of university management and funders, providing as it did potential overlap with fields such as ecology, biology, agriculture, horticulture, all of which would all be able to bring their own perspectives to plant studies. While I had resigned myself to the fact that the humanities and social sciences had long ago become a postmodern swamp, I was filled with foreboding by the thought that not even the natural sciences were safe from the challenges posed by plant life.

The conversation with my colleague brought forth some buds that had been growing for a while, in particular my unease with a discipline that had been showing distinct signs of hypertrophy for some time. I had noted that for some years now, browsing through programmes of our disciplinary conventions, that one would be lucky to come across an academic paper that mentioned a country or international organisation in its title. There were so many debates about "epistemology" and "ontology" that one could be forgiven for thinking they had stumbled into a philosophy conference.[2] Nor were those who cast themselves in the mould of scientists much better. Among so-called scientists, debates rapidly degenerated into atheoretical discussions about the competing merits of various econometric techniques whose growing sophistication and complexity was in inverse proportion to the intellectual fruits yielded by these efforts. These so-called scientists' faculties of reason and analysis had been degraded by scholastic discussions of statistical appropriateness and "hacks" for manipulating software packages – a vision of political science as a conjurer's bag of tricks. Political scientists in IR now incarnated a kind of liberal rationalist utopianism, out of kilter with changing political realities. Skilled at predicting the past, their incantations were appropriate for the receding liberal technocratic era in which the basic questions of political order were all assumed to be safely settled, thereby allowing the econometric predictions to safely proliferate. They were, in effect, yet another caste of postmodern high priests, whose mastery of statistical esotericism was intended to ward off politics, not to understand it. This was, in short, a regression to a state of "pre-theory."[3] Tightly hugging the stony ground of mid-range theory, behaviourist and neo-positivist approaches carefully insulated themselves from larger claims about the changing character of international order or competition for power.

Given how deeply rooted these problems were, I realised that a radical critique was required, and, as Karl Marx points out, to be radical means to grasp things by the root. In a post-patriarchal age, what could be more radical than to return to one of the founding fathers of the IR discipline, Edward Hallett Carr? By an uncanny coincidence, on the eve of the eightieth anniversary of the publication of Carr's classic text *The Twenty Years' Crisis, 1919–1939,* world politics was thick with fears of economic depression, rampant nationalism, renewed geopolitical rivalries, resurgent xenophobia, populist demagogy and portents of cataclysmic international collapse – echoes of the interbellum of 1919 to 1939. What makes Carr's text so useful and apposite however is less the similarities between our time and his as the fact that he shows how the internal contradictions of interwar liberalism rent it apart. In other words, Carr's insights should spur us not to misapportion blame for our woes on external foes. Carr also went further than this, charging inter-war liberalism with being utopian, as the liberals of his era frantically sought to maintain and propagate the outmoded ideals and institutions of earlier eras deep into the twentieth century. In this book, I argue that new and vigorous strains of liberal utopianism have emerged that are no less deeply rooted in existing power structures, that, confusingly, take anti-liberal forms but that are no less effective in obscuring the realities of international politics. I want to show that Carr's critique can be usefully applied to help us see how so many of our ideas, theories, and concepts about international politics serve existing interests while expressing the outlook of an era that is receding into history – unipolar globalization.

These thoughts came to me from engaging with Carr scholars. At an international conference at the University of Kent held in November 2017, IR theorist Kevork Oskanian pointed out that renewed geopolitical rivalry in Eastern Europe had been inadvertently rekindled by a liberal ingenuousness about political power that was akin to the naive inter-war liberalism criticized by Carr. Oskanian made the case that, much like Carr's analysis of the "have-not" powers of the inter-war period, Russia's resurgence could be seen as a revolt against a flawed peace settlement, this one stemming from the end of the Cold War rather than the Great War.[4]

Yet neither were the parallels so straightforward. At the same conference, I presented a paper in which I argued that, against the expectations offered up in Carr's book, it was the Western states, and not Russia, that were the leading revisionist powers. That is, it was the satisfied powers of the Western world led by the US – those who benefitted the most from the contemporary international order – that were, bizarrely, using force to revise that order, thereby destabilising the very foundations of their own power.[5] I realised at this point that identifying the contrasts between Carr's time and ours could be as fruitful as identifying the similarities. It also began to dawn on me that Carr's critique of inter-war liberalism could be applied far beyond the blunders and hypocrisies of the European Union (EU) and NATO expansion in Eastern Europe. I also realised that more could be done with Carr's critique than merely inverting it.

When I read Carr as an undergraduate and then re-read him as a postgraduate in Carr's own institution at Aberystwyth in Wales, I had naively imagined that his invocation of a liberal utopianism that cemented together statesmen, scholars, and international lawyers in a single edifice was a thoroughly artificial mock-up, a cardboard cut-out quickly thrown up for polemical purposes that now had, at best, only heuristic value. In any case, by the time I started my university studies, Carr was outdated. Indeed, the very idea that there had ever been a grand debate in which Carr had cut down the tendrils and creepers of liberal utopianism was now considered passé.[6] Thus I never imagined that such utopianism would be so thickly rooted and prodigiously grown in my own lifetime – that there would be such a powerful and destructive commitment to self-evidently flawed and failing projects such as the Eurozone; that there would be a pathological attachment to fighting wars to mitigate human suffering despite a ruinous legacy of permanent war as its result; or that there would be a determined attempt by liberals in the UK to thwart the outcomes of mass politics by seeking to overturn the Brexit vote of 2016. When Carr derided US president Woodrow Wilson for saying of the League of Nations that, "If it won't work, it must be made to work," he could have just as easily been criticizing the utterances of Mario Draghi, the former president of the European Central Bank who oversaw the Eurozone debt crisis from 2011 to 2019. They and others asserted a utopianism of the liberal status quo because the alternative to the status quo was cast as so unconscionably terrible that they simply could not consider it.[7] In short, while I was unsurprised by the sluggish pace of political change in the face of new realities, naively I never expected that there would be such a strongly dogmatic *intellectual* refusal to accept and adapt to new political realities – a refusal to accept the consequences of restless mass politics for the structure and shape of international order.

In the *Twenty Years' Crisis*, Carr had approvingly quoted V.I. Lenin's assertion that "Politics begins where the masses are, not where there are thousands, but where there are millions, that is where serious politics begins."[8] Yet in the aftermath of the Brexit vote, I realised that to hold this view in the British academy today was akin to being a vicar in the Church of England who was actually religious and not merely spiritual. That is, to have such a view of politics was considered to be extremely impolite, if not indeed heretical. Brexit lit up all the most basic questions of international politics – the character of international cooperation, the meaning of sovereignty, the appeal of self-determination, the character of nationalism. The reaction to it made clear the difficulties we had in comprehending change, and the fact that IR scholars had grown accustomed to looking to Brussels and New York as their preferred sites of politics – places where politics was safely boosted out of the reach of the masses. Judging by Carr's text, the politicians, diplomats, scholars, and theorists of his day were similarly hostile towards mass politics. How was it that the academy and its international relations specialists had remained in the same place, despite the intervening eighty years of twentieth-century and twenty-first-century history, the massification of higher education across that period, and the shift in its centre of gravity leftwards? Could it be that the liberal utopianism that Carr excoriated back in 1939 still prevailed in the study of international affairs?

Thus, while it had long been clear to me that far too much of contemporary international studies was, as Carr put it back in his own day, "bankrupt," "sterile," "glib," "gullible," a "hollow and intolerable sham,"[9] it was only after the events of 2016 that I began to wonder whether despite all the colourful variegation, those dense thickets of contemporary IR theory were growing in the same soil as the liberal utopianism that Carr had so thoroughly and savagely hacked away at all those decades ago. Indeed, our situation was, if anything, worse, because we seem to have allowed the path hacked by Carr to become overgrown behind our backs. How did we allow utopianism in international affairs to grow back again, and to obscure the intellectual trail that got us here in the first place? This despite the fact that we were nearly a century ahead of Carr and supposedly wiser, more cynical, and experienced following the history of the twentieth century, not to mention the fact that so many of our new utopian internationalists would doubtless themselves have learned of Carr's critique in their undergraduate and postgraduate courses at some of the best universities in the world. Whereas once upon a time every IR undergraduate would have learned about how Carr had trampled the inter-war idealists into the dirt and thereby laid the ground for a more lucid if cynical perspective on international politics, today it has become part of a new IR lore that the "first great debate" was nothing more than a myth.[10] Be that as it may, it seems to me that if there was no first great debate, then it is high time that we had at least some debate, if not a great one.

Part of the reason we are lost in this jungle is that the political science that Carr sought to establish – realism – has been allowed to wither in the British academy, whereas the new liberal utopians – critical theorists, constructivists, feminists, neo-positivists, among others – do not see themselves as such, despite having their roots deeply planted in the soil of unipolar, US-led globalization. While British IR has produced some intricate, beautiful, and delicate blossoms over the last few decades, the hard task of clearing the liberal-utopian undergrowth has largely been undertaken by strong-armed American realists such as Andrew Bacevich, John J. Mearsheimer, and Stephen M. Walt, who have hacked away at the dense foliage of liberal idealism, which has ensnared Western states in permanent war and left a trail of bloody ruination across the Greater Middle East. Mearsheimer and Walt see what they call "liberal hegemony" as a kind of military Keynesianism for US intellectuals, "a full-employment strategy for the foreign policy establishment." That employment, entailing nation-building, perpetual peace processes, democratization, diffusing human rights, and justifying permanent war have all proved to be labour-intensive rather than intellectually-intensive enterprises.[11]

The British IR establishment is also predicated on liberal hegemony, however much it may resent or deny it. Yet how could it be that a discipline that is in so many ways hostile to the basic tenets of political liberalism – deeply suspicious of national self-determination, state sovereignty, liberal capitalism, markets – could flourish in what is said to be a "liberal international order"? Liberal internationalism itself has also been turned inside out with remarkably little comment, as liberals have switched from supporting self-determination to supporting supranationalism, from national independence to interdependence, and, most strikingly of all, from peace to war.[12] Examining this paradox requires more than slashing at "liberal hegemony" – it requires us to also understand why mutant intellectual growths that look so different from, and frequently much more bizarre than, those in Carr's day nonetheless produce the same kind of liberal entanglements to trap the unwary. In his critique of liberal hegemony, Mearsheimer puts Carr to one side for Carr's supposedly restrictive focus on British imperial utilitarianism, a doctrine long since abandoned.[13] I think this is not only too hasty but also a truncated view of Carr's critique – and that there is much that we can still relearn from Carr. For Carr helps us to see that it is liberal utopianism and not merely liberal hegemony that is the problem, as visible in the liberal insistence on ruling out political alternatives to the status quo. Despite Carr's influence on an earlier generation of American IR theorists such as Hans J. Morgenthau, Robert Gilpin and Stanley Hoffmann, today the US academy tends to overlook Carr in favour of Morgenthau, George F. Kennan, and Reinhold Niebuhr.[14] It is high time that British IR reclaimed Carr's intellectual patrimony, and used it to unsettle the complacent status quo of critical IR orthodoxy. If American IR is perhaps slowly emerging from the jungle of permanent war, can British IR find its own path? I hope this book will help us to do so.

Mearsheimer and Walt use realist theory to criticise the humanitarian idealism of US foreign policy that has led to the age of permanent war. I want to use Carr to take us further than the critique of US foreign policy. For Carr does not simply assert the abiding significance of political power and state interests – he shows how institutions and ideas are plugged into and express underlying power structures, and how liberal utopianism provides a hard ideological carapace for liberal hegemony. This is how I want to deploy Carr in this book. We shall see that once marginalised, now dominant heterodox theories turned out to be eminently well adapted to serve the needs and interests of existing power structures. It is Carr's critique of liberal idealism that will take us past the critique of US foreign policy to the critique of European politics, that realm of supposed peace and prosperity, allowing us to razor apart what I style as "Eutopianism" in the third chapter. As should be evident, this book was written under the political pressure of Brexit, Britain's tortuous effort to extricate itself from the structures of the EU since 2016. As this is a book about political change in international politics and how it is theorized, Brexit Britain offers an exultant vantage point from which to observe and try to understand these changes. How far immersion in the moment helps to sharpen the insights in this book is for the reader to judge, but the moment itself was highly propitious for analysing the changing international order. Had the book been written under different circumstances it would undoubtedly have been a different book, but not necessarily a better one.

I would like to extend my thanks to the School of Politics and International Relations at the University of Kent for kindly offering the financial support that enabled this manuscript to be completed at such a furious pace. I would also like to thank Richard Baggaley, my editor at McGill-Queens' University Press, for being enthusiastic about the project from the start and for his patience with the process of completing it. In addition to the workshop at the University of Kent already mentioned, the discussion in the book also benefitted from participating in the "Europe after Brexit" conference organised by Professor Costas Lapavitsas at the School of Oriental and African Studies in September 2018, from a seminar with Professor Wolfgang Streeck held at the LSE in March 2019, as well as the lecture delivered by Professor Streeck that same evening, and last but not least a roundtable on the continuing relevance of E.H. Carr that I convened at the annual conference of the British International Studies Association in London in June 2019. A special note of thanks is also due to those who read the manuscript and provided critical feedback, namely (and in no particular order): Daniel Matthews-Ferrero, Rubrick Biegon, Tim Aistrope, Daniel Dunleavy, Charles Devellennes, Keith Smith and two anonymous reviewers working on behalf of the publisher.

They all have my gratitude for sharpening my thinking about questions of contemporary world politics. Needless to say, any and all errors of fact and judgement are mine alone. The book is dedicated to my nephew, Mio, in the hope that the twenty years' crisis will finally have ended by the time he reaches manhood.

Canterbury
December 2019

The New Twenty Years' Crisis

Introduction: Willing the End

International relations is, by common assent, in serious trouble. Trade wars threaten to fragment the global economy, damaging business, supply chains, and economic growth and perhaps even knocking globalization into reverse – the prospect of "de-globalization." Geopolitical rivalry between great powers is sharper than it has been for a generation, fracturing not only the Middle East and South China Sea, but even Europe itself, with war simmering in Ukraine. The US scorns climate change agreements and nuclear arms reduction treaties, while both Russia and the US are seeking to modernize their vast stockpiles of nuclear weapons. The European Union (EU) is subject to powerful centrifugal forces, as divergence between its northern core and southern periphery strains against the integument of the Eurozone, and populist and radical right challengers joust with liberals to determine the future of the continent. Looming above and beyond all of this is also the prospect of ecological degradation, climatic collapse, and, not least, pandemic disease.

It is not just the scale of these challenges that makes them appear so formidable, but also the fact that they explicitly break with the norms, institutions, and mores of the prevailing era of liberal internationalism. China has constructed an open *and* state-dominated capitalist economy under an authoritarian one-party system, pioneering new technologies of mass population control, thereby resisting the logic of both political liberalization and democratization. The radical right populists of Central and Eastern Europe have built their appeal and power not on following the regimens of global economic agencies, but through state intervention and authority built around invoking nationalism, the family, and traditional religion, oftentimes in express defiance of global and continental mores of minority rights and sexual and ethnic diversity, as well as economic orthodoxy.[1] Taken together, all these intersecting trends seem deeply threatening to an international order founded on an interlocking system of open, integrated economies bound together through trade networks and financial flows; overseen by supranational institutions devised for the collective management of interests at the regional, international, and global levels; managed by transnational courts and regulatory agencies, with an unstable but remote periphery policed by multinational armies of blue helmets in small-scale bush wars; and cemented by norms and value systems that are no less expansive and transcendent – supranational authority, universal human rights, international and transnational law, multiculturalism.

Inevitably, these challenges have prompted comparisons with the interbellum of 1919 to 1939 – that period between the two world wars in which the liberal international order constructed through the postwar Paris Peace Treaties crumbled away. Now, as then, world politics is snarled up in the long tail of a global slump while the international order confronts centrifugal pressures of resurgent nationalism and tense geopolitical rivalry. No liberal solutions appear to be left, and our collective capacity to inaugurate "peaceful change" in the face of new rising powers seems decidedly precarious, not least because the Trump administration seems to have jettisoned the strategy of "socializing" China into the international order.[2] A new generation of charismatic leaders has emerged heading up populist and radical right parties, storming the citadels of power. As the colours swirl more darkly, it only takes a few more strokes of the brush and, all too quickly, sure enough the picture before us looks grimly familiar: depression, expansionist nationalism, wars over resources, geopolitical tension, fascism, and emerging through all the murk and gloom, the final collapse of international order, war, and genocide.

International Relations (IR), the academic study of these phenomena of international relations is, I aver, also in serious trouble, albeit less remarked upon than the problems confronting the world system. Yet the scholarly difficulty is not merely incidental to "real world problems" because the intellectual difficulty compounds the practical one. For how will we conceive robust, informed responses to our problems if we have difficulty understanding them for what they are? I will argue that our contemporary intellectual and political problems can at least be usefully diagnosed by revisiting some canonical texts and frameworks in the discipline rather than assuming that we have advanced beyond them simply by virtue of being more advanced in time. More than this, I would argue that some of our fundamental problems remain the same as theirs, and in particular that the utopianism diagnosed by Carr in the interbellum remains deeply embedded in our current paradigms and theories. While Carr diagnosed a collective identity shared across a fairly compact cadre of Western thinkers, policy makers, analysts, and political leaders, I suggest that today an ostensibly more disparate elite nonetheless shares common assumptions, outlooks, and dispositions that bind them together.[3] Thus I contend that the old liberal utopian strains have evolved into exotic new hybrid varieties.

In particular, I want to argue that what Carr diagnosed as utopianism is now evident not only among liberals, as Carr claimed back in 1939, but especially among IR critical scholars, broadly conceived.[4] While there is plenty of debate about what constitutes Critical IR, I do not intend to spend much time unpicking these arguments. Many of these debates tend to be dominated by the narcissism of petty differences, and in any case one of the central claims of this book is that what unifies Critical IR is the fact that, whatever its prodigious and wondrous intellectual variety, it shares a common taproot of liberal utopianism, deeply sunk into the soil of unipolar globalization. Thus, eighty years after Carr excoriated the discipline for its lack of intellectual progress and primitive scientific understanding, it seems that we have not advanced very far. Indeed, Carr's critique of the frustrated liberals of his day still rings uncannily true today:

> The bankruptcy of utopianism resides not in its failure to live up to its principles, but in the exposure of its inability to provide any absolute and disinterested standard for the conduct of international affairs. The utopian, faced by the collapse of standards whose interested character he has failed to penetrate, takes refuge in condemnation of a reality which refuses to conform to these standards.[5]

Who cannot but see the echoes of this in the veritable derangement that greeted Britain's vote to leave the EU and the election of Donald Trump as US president in 2016? How else could the liberal and left responses to these events seem, except as a flight from political reality – seeking refuge, as Carr puts it, in condemnation of the reality that fails to fit their preconceived standards? The deep attachment of critical scholars to the prevailing liberal order stood exposed.

What Carr diagnosed as utopianism is still the "political unconscious" of much of contemporary IR, in which genuine but dimly perceived political and social problems are misdiagnosed, if ever even acknowledged, and then systematically evaded through impotent intellectual churning and theoretical flux. So while the development of constructivist and critical approaches over the last several decades may have allowed the discipline of IR to snap the contrastive textbook manacles of liberalism and realism, we have not, I argue, escaped utopianism.

How then did Carr diagnose utopianism? Carr's diagnosis of utopianism is at once sweeping and subtle and thus can only be summarised with difficulty. Nonetheless, we can pick out some inter-related features that can help us identify utopianism today.[6] First, utopianism is characterised by substituting wishful thinking for factual analysis. While Carr was intelligent enough to know that purpose inevitably conditions all analysis, he maintained that our purposes can only gain traction if they are aligned with reality. "Purpose," Carr suggested, "which should logically follow analysis, is required to give it both its initial impulse and its direction."[7] Instead, Carr charged utopianism with "paying too little attention to existing 'facts' or to the analysis of cause and effect [instead devoting] themselves wholeheartedly to the elaboration of visionary projects for the attainment of the ends which they have in view – projects whose simplicity and perfection give them an easy and universal appeal."[8] Of all these visionary projects, perhaps none is so powerful and beguiling in the contemporary world as the European Union – but that is getting ahead of the argument. Flowing from this is the second problem, that utopianism is characterised by the "almost total neglect of the factor of power."[9] To be sure, power is not everything but "it is safe to say that power is always an essential element in politics."[10] To miss how power plays out in politics is thus to entirely misconceive politics itself. Third, this means that power conditions all our perspectives, and that frank acknowledgement of this conditioned and historically relative character of our thinking is a keystone of scientific thought – a point that, as we shall see, is as lost on those claiming the mantle of science as much as it is on everyone else.

The fourth prototypical characteristic of utopian thinking and one that is quintessentially liberal is the notion of the "harmony of interests" – that doctrine that sees all peoples' and nations' interests as fundamentally compatible, with political conflict being only the passing friction of these divergent interests being brought into their supposedly natural alignment. Whereas the state could use its power to force the political convergence of interests within the domestic sphere, it was precisely the absence of such centralised power in the international sphere that makes the prospect of harmony in the international sphere all the more enchanting, according to Carr.[11] That this classically liberal doctrine of nineteenth-century international politics should have survived and been recreated in new forms precisely by those who thought that they had superseded liberalism in our century, is one of the most intriguing puzzles of our contemporary international order, and will be addressed in greater detail in chapter 3, when we consider the utopian characteristics of European integration.

Carr noted that the core condition for the success of the doctrine of the "harmony of interests" across the nineteenth century was the "unparalleled expansion of production, population and prosperity, which marked the hundred years following the publication of *The Wealth of Nations* and the invention of the steam engine."[12] The First World War finally brought this halcyon era to an end – an event that also entirely restructured Carr's hitherto complacent outlook of Victorian liberalism. Today, too, the "tacit presupposition of infinitely expanding markets" was the foundation of new forms of liberal utopianism, our own "unparalleled expansion" being powered by the industrialization of East Asia and the accompanying boom in global trade since the end of the Cold War. For all the cavilling against "neoliberalism" in the academy, neoliberal globalization under US leadership has been the economic precondition for critical hegemony in the academy. Critical theories, including Critical IR, are part of the left wing of neoliberalism – what the political theorist Nancy Fraser called "progressive neoliberalism."[13]

The fifth feature of utopianism identified by Carr is that the espousal of inter-war liberalism reflected the interests of the status quo powers, Britain, France, and the US. As our twenty years' crisis has come to an end, it is striking to see the US now abandoning the policies of liberal hegemony that it had pursued since the end of the Cold War, most notably in its attempt to stoke a trade war with China, the restructuring of the North American Free Trade Agreement (NAFTA) and the strategic withdrawal from Europe, and its response to the COVID-19 viral pandemic. The rising power, China, meanwhile, seeks the mantle of liberal international leadership, claiming to stand for an open global system based on free trade principles, as well as taking the lead in the deployment of United Nations peacekeepers. As the liberal international order decays, according to Carr's logic, its vacuity will become more glaring as it comes to be increasingly exposed as an a priori construct of abstractly rational notions that bear no resemblance to reality. This last feature is most evident, as we shall see in chapter 3, in the fanatical commitment to perpetuate the European Union against the disintegrative forces gnawing away on its insides. In the last twist, "If mankind in its international relations had signally failed to achieve the rational good," Carr notes, then the utopian retreats to the conclusion that people "must either have been too stupid to understand good, or too wicked to pursue it."[14] One need only look to the scorn heaped on Brexit and its supporters, or Emmanuel Macron's vicious denunciation of the *gilets jaunes*, to see how this liberal utopian dynamic continues today.

It is worth stressing that Carr took the liberal internationalism associated with US president Woodrow Wilson and his League of Nations as the exemplar of utopianism. It seemed self-evident to Carr that, since the conditions for liberal internationalism no longer prevailed by the late 1930s, so too attachment to the prior liberal international order was vain and absurd. This is why his theory is so challenging and intriguing for us today – because one of the defining characteristics of contemporary liberalism is its insistent pragmatism and explicitly *anti-*utopian character. The appeal of post-Cold War liberalism was that it was anti-totalitarian, having ostensibly been vindicated by the implosion of the Soviet bloc.[15] That was a liberalism that was cast *against* the vain utopian search for political and social perfection – a search which had imposed such a terrible cost in the last century, as a complex human reality was brutally shorn to fit an idealized Procrustian framework. Today the prototypical form of utopianism is still taken to be the totalitarian regimes of the twentieth century, whose search for flawlessness cost humanity so much, with the implicit warning that deviation from technocratic political centrism will inevitably lead to cataclysm.

Yet today the liberal international order is degrading once again, and once again political reality is developing in ways that escape our preconceived notions of the ideal international order inherited from the 1990s. Having imagined ourselves so much wiser and more mature than the bloody delusional utopians of the twentieth century, we still cling to liberal forms that are increasingly utopian because they fail to fit with the emerging shape of the new order of fraught global trade and geopolitical competition. It is this that makes revisiting Carr's critique so worthwhile. Carr's supple dialectic captured the contortions of liberal utopianism as it degrades from universalism to particularlism, with the liberal utopian first claiming "that what is best for the world is best for his country, and then [reversing] the argument to read that what is best for his country is best for the world, the two propositions being, from the utopian standpoint, identical."[16] This has been the pattern for the globalizing liberalism of the last several decades as Western states have obliviously promoted policies of democratization, humanitarianism, and free trade – reliant on an "unconscious cynicism" that their interests were the same as everyone else's – a cynicism that was a "far more effective diplomatic weapon than the deliberate and self-conscious cynicism" of old-fashioned realpolitik.[17] The final contortion of liberal utopianism is to resolve itself in impotent moralizing, as the liberal utopian, "faced by the collapse of standards whose interested character he has failed to penetrate, takes refuge in condemnation of a reality which refuses to conform to these standards."[18] This flight from reality can be seen in the self-serving fables so prevalent among our latter-day utopians, such as the persistent belief that the global political realignment we are witnessing is the outcome of pure contingency and thus easily reversed – the hubristic whim of British prime minister David Cameron in calling a national referendum on the EU, or a few thousand votes in northeastern rustbelt constituencies that won Donald Trump the US Electoral College, Russian secret agents' manipulation of social media, or a mutant virus escaping from a wet market in Wuhan ... But there are too many such intersecting coincidences to be random: we know that it is politics itself that is changing.

Liberal centrists such as the French president Emmanuel Macron or those who still wish to reverse Brexit years after the referendum, insist on their fundamental pragmatism, arguing that there is simply no conscionable alternative to their propositions – and it is precisely in this insistence on the lack of alternatives that their ideological utopianism is so plainly revealed. Slavoj Žižek helps explain this paradox:

> the supreme irony [is that] as it functions today, ideology appears as its exact opposite, as a radical critique of ideological utopias. The predominant ideology now is not a positive vision of some utopian future but a cynical resignation, an acceptance of how "the world really is," accompanied by a warning that if we want to change it too much, only totalitarian horror will ensue. Every vision of another world is dismissed as ideology [...] the main function of ideological censorship today is not to crush actual resistance ... but to crush hope, immediately to denounce every critical project as opening a path at the end of which is ... a gulag.[19]

As Žižek suggests, the utopianism of post-Cold War liberalism lies in the refusal to countenance self-consciously directed positive improvement. As the status quo changes *of its own accord*, this refusal resolves itself into a hostility to change itself, with liberalism eventually collapsing into a dogmatic attachment to the status quo ante, in which the liberal international order is the best of all possible worlds precisely because it is anti-utopian. As Samuel Moyn has argued, the era of cosmopolitan globalization and human rights turned out to be the Last Utopia – the utopia to which we collectively turned after having exhausted all the others, naively imagining that we had no illusions left while committing to the illusion that the status quo of the post-Cold War era could be sustained and preserved indefinitely.

If Carr's hostility to liberalism makes him exceptionally useful to us today as the liberal international order degrades, by the same token his anti-liberalism also carries a historic warning. Carr's hostility to liberalism led him to be over-impressed by the solidity and power of the totalitarian regimes of his own era, especially the Soviet Triceratops whose power belied the rot within, as so brilliantly evoked by John L. Gaddis:

> [with] its sheer size, tough skin, bristling armament, and aggressive posturing, the beast looked ... formidable .... Appearances deceived, though, for within its digestive, circulatory, and respiratory systems were slowly clogging up, and then shutting down. There were few external signs of this until the day the creature was found with all four feet in the air, still awesome but now bloated, stiff, and quite dead. The moral of the fable is that armaments make impressive exoskeletons, but a shell alone ensures the survival of no animal and no state.[20]

Carr was no by no means the only serious analyst to be overawed by the totalitarian political megafauna of the twentieth century (although there were, to be sure, other contemporaneous political realists, such as George F. Kennan, whose predictions for the USSR proved more accurate than Carr's). Thus, just as much as we can (re)learn from Carr how to identify the liberal utopian character of our contemporary political order, we would be just as wise to consider the other side of the intellectual ledger as well. After having completed the final volume in his monumental history of the USSR, Carr died in 1982, only three years before Mikhail Gorbachev became general secretary of the Soviet Communist Party, and ten years before Gorbachev would preside over the dissolution of the USSR and the end of the Cold War, leading to a new liberal international order so expansive and resurgent that it would come to be seen as post-historic, beyond challenge or contestation ... at any rate, until the crash of 2008.[21] All of this to say that we can also learn from Carr *not* to overstate the strength and durability of challenges to the liberal order. However powerful and imposing Xi's China may appear at the moment, however inexorable the growth of radical right voting blocs and populist parties within the Western world, however cunning Russian president Vladimir Putin, Carr offers us a shadowy mirror in which many things appear that may be usefully considered.

Given the scale and depth of the political changes that we are witnessing, perhaps it is unfair to pick out IR in particular as the one social science discipline that is so at fault. After all, IR and its various ancillary and flanking sub-disciplines suffer from all the maladies that afflict the contemporary university system in the Anglo-American world. These include but are not restricted to academic autonomy being eroded by a growing caste of professionalized administrators, the professionalization of intellectual life and scholarly work, the substitution of reified metrics of careerist advancement in place of scientific progress and evaluative judgement, as well as the enervating and vicious campus culture wars that leave bitterness, recrimination, and censorship in their wake. Nor is IR the only academic discipline struggling to frame and grasp the crisis of liberal international order over the last decade. The discipline of economics, for instance, suffered a tremendous blow to its credibility in 2008. Despite having the benefit of eight years to prepare for the political repercussions of the economic crisis, political scientists were no less stunned as a series of unlikely political changes happened in quick succession. Centrist hegemony was shattered in Britain's Labour Party with the unlikely election of Jeremy Corbyn as its leader in 2015. Britain voted to leave the EU in 2016 and Donald Trump stood against the elite of his own party, the Republicans, and shredded not one but two powerful political families – the Bushes and Clintons – to seize the White House that same year. The year ended with Matteo Renzi, the would-be Italian Tony Blair, humiliatingly losing a constitutional referendum on which he had wagered the liberal centrist future of Italy. The liberalization and democratization of the ex-authoritarian states of the Eastern Bloc, long since stalled, now seemed to be going into reverse, belying the providential character of global democratization. The grand old social democratic parties of Western Europe – mainstays of capitalist democracy since the nineteenth century no less – were eclipsed by radical right populists and liberal competitors in three major European democracies – Italy, France, and Germany.

Yet the academic study of both economics and political science has shown some capacity and will for intellectual adaptation and renewal. The political scientist Matthew Goodwin fulfilled a promise to eat his book live on air as a result of failing to predict the political strength of the Labour Party's showing in the 2017 UK general election – a de facto act of symbolic contrition on behalf of the discipline as a whole. The shocks of Brexit and the election of Donald Trump as US president prompted a year of introspection over the merits and successes of political predictions and polling. Some political theorists claimed to have already occupied that terrain, having forged ahead already, citing Richard Rorty's uncanny prediction from twenty years earlier anticipating the rise of an anti-liberal populism led by a new generation of charismatic leaders, as well as critical theorists' analyses of the "authoritarian personality."[22]

Yet IR should have been ahead of political theory, political science, and economics by 2008, and certainly by 2016. For if there was a single year that would have prompted IR scholars and theorists to an equivalent moment of intellectual reckoning, that year should have been 2003, a full five years before the global economic crisis struck, and thirteen years before Brexit and Hillary Clinton's electoral defeat. In 2003, the US and UK invaded Iraq and together would accomplish the difficult task of leaving that country worse off on virtually every conceivable metric than it had been under the dictatorship of Saddam Hussein – no mean feat, given Saddam's dismal record of wanton cruelty and strategic miscalculation as well as the devastation wrought by the UN sanctions regime against the country.[23] The year 2003 should have been the year that the discipline of IR could vindicate the significance of a global perspective on politics and helped us to discern the outline of the future – that is, our present. The inability of the US to militarily subjugate a country as supine as Iraq combined with the US failure to corral its core allies into supporting the war politically (let alone economically, as with the first Iraq War of 1990–91), US troops and aircraft being denied transit rights even through Turkey, a US government pursuing sweeping tax cuts in the midst of a ruinously expensive omnidirectional war on terror while refusing to rally US society to even a symbolic collective sacrifice, US military reliance on overstretched reservists supported by a vast private army of mercenaries and ethnic death squads to conduct its war, the breakdown of relations with China and Russia on the UN Security Council, Chinese encroachment on Iraq's oilfields that were originally supposed to have been used to pay for the US war effort, the breakdown in trust between politicians and voters in Britain precipitated by the lies over Iraq's weapons of mass destruction – all of these could have been taken as harbingers of change in the broad contours of the international order, with significant ramifications for domestic politics in terms of US national finances and electoral shifts.[24] Instead, Iraq became the alibi for the discipline. With virtually every scholar in the discipline self-righteously opposed to the

Iraq War while proving incapable of analysing it, we thus felt collectively exonerated from thinking any more deeply about the problems confronting the discipline or indeed international order more broadly.

The year 2019 represented a concatenation of significant anniversaries for the discipline. First and foremost, 2019 was the hundredth anniversary of the end of the First World War, which heralded the first attempt to build a liberal international order under US leadership, as well as institutionalizing the world's first formal state-based international organization, the ill-fated League of Nations. That same year saw the institutional launch of the discipline of international relations with the founding of an academic chair devoted to its study in the Welsh seaside resort town of Aberystwyth, at the prompting and under the guidance of the Welsh industrialist, philanthropist, and Liberal politician Lord David Davies. The chair was named for US president Woodrow Wilson, political demiurge of the interwar liberal order. The third significant anniversary for our purposes here is, of course, the fact that 2019 was the eightieth anniversary of the publication of *The Twenty Years' Crisis* by E.H. Carr, who occupied the Woodrow Wilson Chair in Aberystwyth at the time. Carr's polemic diagnosed the disintegration of the order that Woodrow Wilson had sought to build and, in a stroke of genius, he adopted the word "realism" to describe his own outlook in opposition to what he took as the hollow pieties and naivety of the Wilsonian era. With this polemical, highly tendentious bifurcation, Carr established two ideational poles that would help structure debate in the discipline for at least fifty years. Carr's critical diagnosis of the decline of the liberal international order became a foundational text for the post-war discipline. This book is addressed to the consideration of these three anniversaries with the hope that it will help to force an intellectual reckoning and to clear some of the clouds of mystification that have enveloped international politics. Before we begin that task, let us briefly consider why 2003 did not prompt a reorientation in the discipline, which might in turn have intellectually prepared us for more recent shocks.

The Great Alibi

Opposition to the Iraq War was the great alibi of the profession and the discipline. This is visible in the discipline's proclivity towards war despite everything that happened in Iraq. Even the world's premier living philosopher of war, Michael Walzer, opposed intervening in Iraq. Opposing intervention in Iraq has given IR theorists the moral credit to support variants and combinations of military intervention, democratization, and nation-building ever since: in Libya (2011), Côte d'Ivoire (2011), Syria (2011), Mali (2013), and then Iraq again (2014), when the cosmopolitan forces of the Islamic State emerged from underneath the ruins of the Iraqi and Syrian nation-states. At the time of writing, there is the distinct sound of war drums not too far off in the distance as the Trump administration and its Latin American allies politically interfere in Venezuelan politics and US aircraft carriers are despatched to menace Iran.

The discipline as a whole is deeply, viscerally, and ideologically committed to war: it has facilitated a public culture in the Western world that is now accustomed to permanent war. The depth of this commitment should never be underestimated. It is greater than that found in any defence ministry – and certainly more than among old-fashioned realists. If that sounds extreme, consider the volume of theories pumped out by international relations scholars arguing for military intervention. Indeed, the archetypal model of liberal warfare – military intervention to defend human rights and relieve human suffering – was a theory primarily formulated and propounded by academics and even philosophers. It is difficult to think of an analogue in other disciplines to match the ferocious commitment to war in IR. There are, to be sure, economists who support austerity as a route to economic recovery and growth, and those who see "creative destruction" as part of the process of rebooting economies through recession. Yet I know of no economist committed to permanent crisis as a good, or (with the possible exception of certain green economists) who urges the institutionalization of austerity and negative growth as a permanent feature of economic life.[25] Among political scientists there are plenty who believe that the membership of the EU is compatible with representative government, but you would have to go back to the 1960s to find political scientists openly arguing for dictatorship as necessary to political development.[26] In short, there is no discipline that is as committed as IR is to the most destructive and violent aspects of its objects of study.

A commitment to permanent war is part of the "liberal hegemony" dissected by Stephen Walt and John J. Mearsheimer. Certainly, there were those who opposed liberal intervention in the discipline before these two American IR theorists, but they were decidedly a minority and were disparaged as "Chomskyites" and "Marxists." There were also plenty of disputes over the modalities of specific interventions – such as how important the support of regional organizations is – yet there were very few who were willing to condemn intervention *tout court*. Critical theorists, as with all left-leaning liberals, were always susceptible to the guilt-inducing demand to come up with alternatives. Alternatives in this case usually meant supporting multilateralism as opposed to uni-lateralism, the UN as opposed to coalitions of the willing, the respons-ibility to protect instead of humanitarian intervention, hybrid peace to liberal peace, traditional justice to transnational justice, elders and tribal councils (supported by NGOs of course) to liberal democracy, blue helmets to marines. Feminist Sandra Whitworth, for instance, fiercely critical of the derelictions of militarized UN peacekeeping in Africa, promoted in its stead an expansive vision of nation-building, urging the despatch of "contingents of doctors, feminists, linguists, and engineers; regiments of construction workers and carpenters; armies of midwives, cultural critics, anthropologists and social work-ers; battalions of artists, musicians, poets, writers and social critics."[27] The US military took up the suggestion at least with anthropologists, with its notorious "Human Terrain System" becoming an embedded part of the war on terror in Afghanistan and Iraq. Even the US army, it seems, has gone critical.

Those who may have felt queasy about bombing Africans and Arabs could always be relied upon to support bombing Europeans, especially if they were from the Balkans. If critical scholars had compunctions about crusades to spread human rights in Africa and the Islamic world, they had no compunctions about despatching German warplanes and soldiers back to the Balkans, despite the legacy of brutal Nazi con-quest in the region. "Why fight?," mused the post-structural IR theor-ist David Campbell in the late 1990s.[28] Lest anyone be concerned, he did indeed find sufficient reasons, as did many other critical theorists (or, rather, they found sufficient reasons as to why NATO was in fact fighting on behalf of critical theory).[29] Campbell took his intellectual inspiration from the post-structural philosopher Jacques Derrida, yet he managed to find his way to offering critical support for the humani-tarian protectorate that NATO imposed on Bosnia-Herzegovina, even though it turned out to be justified in liberal humanitarian rather than Derridean terms.[30] Indeed, Campbell disparaged the NATO protect-orate for being *too* liberal, strongly urging the viceroys in Sarajevo to wield their neocolonial powers to crush such errant liberal notions as free speech for the natives.[31]

In short, critique was in short supply. This reflected the unipolar structure of the international system after the end of the Cold War. The costs and risks of war and nation-building were drastically reduced by the implosion of the USSR and collapse of Third World nationalism, as there was no longer any countervailing force capable of politically and militarily checking Western interventionism, or even merely forcing hard-headed pragmatic deliberation about the geopolitical consequences of the use of force, or its impact on local balances of power between ethnic groups within countries, or on strategic relations at the regional and global level. As the UN Security Council was no longer stymied by Cold War rivalries, for liberals and critical theorists the end of the Cold War had the added benefit that Western power could now be bundled up in the blue banner of the United Nations. In practical terms, intervention and nation-building could be safely outsourced to blue helmets in vast new peacebuilding operations, which not only avoided the problem of spending (Western) blood and treasure, but also undercut the need for any clear deliberation about politics and strategy. In inverse proportion to the slashed costs and risks of war and intervention, there was a boom in Western theorising for spreading human rights and democracy. Even the theological, pre-modern casuistry of just war thinking was revived – a sign of sub-realist regression in international theory if ever there was one – as Thomas Aquinas and St Augustine miraculously reappeared in the annals of IR once the Soviet Union had expired, clearing the way for a new ethical militarism.[32]

Unipolarity also qualitatively affected the character of critique. As noted by a senior functionary of the Clinton administration, James Rubin, for a time around the invasion of Iraq the discipline of IR had practically morphed into a discipline of "American empire studies."[33] An enormous upsurge of scholarship took the Bush administration's grandiloquent ambitions at face value, the ideology of an imperial juggernaut intent on plundering fossil fuels and globalizing Western ideals. This was a juggernaut that had grown so mighty and overweening in the eyes of some theorists that it simply became a single, integrated global polity – or *Empire*, as the title of Michael Hardt and Antonio Negri's book would have it.[34] Yet what should have been quickly obvious to any sober observer – that we were witnessing a squalid imperial failure and not the apotheosis of imperial might, and indeed that the brutality and suffering were exacerbated by the *failure* to impose order – all of this should have prompted serious intellectual searching in the discipline. To admit imperial failure however would have been to surrender comforting nostrums that were too dear to critically minded and radical scholars to relinquish – that of American leadership and power. For what was there to say if Western power could not be critiqued? Thus, critical and left-leaning professors turned out to be more attached to US power than even the Pentagon or the State Department.

American empire has been good for IR, if not for the Middle East. Now, not unlike American power itself, the discipline of IR is enormous, sprawling, complacent, conceited, and decadent. Like the US itself, IR has also squandered the last thirty years since the end of the Cold War in failing to prepare for the next stage of international politics now upon us. The last thirty years were the academic golden age of IR, the master's degree in IR being the political complement to the MBA for those whom the critical theorist Robert Cox called the "transnational managerial class" – or at least those who aspired to that role.[35] Both degree systems were designed to provide the framework for managing a globalizing world in which all the basic questions of domestic politics were taken to be settled and sufficiently tightly compressed within a narrow ideological spectrum that they could be safely turned over to supranational authorities and technocrats. The international realm still seemed one in which progressive transformation was possible, even if this activity was essentially an "alignment of the provinces," to paraphrase Alexandre Kojève – diffusing human rights, gender enlightenment, liberal democracy, and global justice to the backward and wayward parts of the world. Masters' courses in terrorism, conflict, security, development, international law, globalization, and peace and conflict studies abounded. For who indeed would want to study domestic politics with the likes of Tony Blair, Jacques Chirac, Lionel Jospin, Gerhard Schröder, or Bill Clinton in charge?

Thus an entire cohort of global middle-class youth who would cross the road to avoid a working-class man were socialized into thinking that all the world's most important problems lay elsewhere – in Palestine, in Rwanda, Nepal, wherever. To that extent, however much "neoliberal globalization" may have been criticised and disparaged on reading lists and in lecture halls, the discipline of IR and its many and varied flanking and subordinated sub-fields were complicit in the premise on which technocratic centrism and neoliberal hegemony were built: that all serious challenges – whether climate change, terrorism, development, ethnic conflict – lay outside and abroad. In this way, an entire generation's energy and dynamism was extended in the activity of aligning the provinces, whether they turned out to be apparatchiks for development and humanitarian NGOs and aid charities, gender advisers to NATO, secret police agents for the war on terror, black bloc anti-globalization protestors trailing after the elite international conference circuit, or, indeed, IR theorists.

As usual, intellectual expansion marched in lock step with imperial expansion. When scholars of critical security studies claimed that "emancipation" was the goal in shifting from state-centred ideas of security to human security, it seemed self-evident that guaranteeing lives and physical integrity was a better thing than focussing on the bogus "national" security needs of the elites in capital cities. In practice, such emancipation provided yet another ideological crowbar for international agencies, NGOs, and Western states to prise open the sovereignty of developing countries. The unipolar imaginary stretches from the mesmerising sublime of the biosphere and new systems theories, right through to the mundane, as the discipline of IR expanded more relentlessly and aggressively than "the Empire" itself. Constantly annexing new domains, IR could be seen as one of the ideological handmaidens of unipolar globalization. Just as globalization taught us that everything could be commodified, IR taught us that nothing was too trivial to be considered irrelevant, no area too remote, no topic too obscure, that it could not be annexed and examined from the global or international point of view. Collections of scholarly essays and research monographs were published on topics such as zombies, "Hello Kitty," Harry Potter, and how they all related to IR.[36] Papers were published in esteemed scholarly periodicals ruminating on the resistance potential of craft beers, while workshops were held to consider domains that had hitherto been overlooked in the discipline, such as colour and sound and their relevance for IR.[37]

What began as tentative forays into broaching the privileged, supposedly "masculine" domain of "high politics" in favour of the ignored, relegated domain of feminine "low politics" powered a remorseless expansion of the discipline: "To adopt a feminist slogan," asserted Ken Booth, "the international is personal and the personal is international."[38] Everything became IR. From the viewpoint of IR theory, there is now nothing so banal, trivial, and vulgar that it cannot be saturated with international significance and endowed with geopolitical meaning. Following the injunction of IR feminist Cynthia Enloe for the discipline to turn its attention to the "mundane," the journal *Millennium* offers up a paper that engages in a "close reading" of a urinal in a Scottish pub – the academic "study" of which is cast as "an explicit political intervention" while modestly conceding that the "act of urinating" will not in itself lead to revolution.[39] Doubtless the paper will probably be criticized in turn as being too patriarchal in its one-sided focus on purely male sanitation objects, even though it acknowledges the inherently exclusionary practices of male micturition.[40] IR is now a discipline that is beyond satire and impossible to hoax, for who would be entitled to say anymore what is a legitimate outer boundary to disciplinary concerns?[41] This is embodied in the most recent turn to "everyday critique" in IR, a move inspired by critical sociology, premised on the claim that scholarly critique is not so different from the practice of ordinary argument by laypeople. Here we have the final conceit of a conceited discipline, the exhausted collapse into banality, in which critical scholars deign to relinquish any privileged objects of analysis or claim to privileged insight. Patronisingly cast as intellectual humility, what it ultimately amounts to is an admission of intellectual defeat.[42]

Thus, within the space of fifteen years, there was no outer limit to the concerns and interests of the discipline. Not unlike Empire itself, everything had become internal to a single overarching hegemonic system. This process of trivialization and banalization had already reached its nadir some years back, at the largest annual congress of IR researchers (and largest annual global gathering of political scientists), the International Studies Association, in the US city of Atlanta in 2016. There, a large and well-attended roundtable was held in which eminent professors came to the discussion dressed as their favourite characters from the film franchise *Star Wars* and television show *Game of Thrones*. Some of these scholars even prepared "teaser trailers" for these panels on YouTube – at the time of writing, they can still be viewed online, peculiar Internet time capsules from the unipolar era of liberal hegemony.[43] One can only imagine how a world congress of economists dressing up as make-believe characters would have appeared to outside observers in 2008. Indeed, one can imagine that those very same IR scholars who played dress-up for their panel in 2016 would have been outraged had, say, oncologists, or social workers, or climate change scientists done the same at one of their own scientific congresses. This specific congress of the International Studies Association happened in March, only months before the Brexit referendum and Trump's victory over Hillary Clinton, both of which would produce veritable derangement in the discipline – a discipline supposedly dedicated to the study of the most brutal, violent, and necessitous form of politics.[44] As the liberal international order degrades and is restructured, it is worth tracing how IR theories become more utopian, its intellectual constructs reflecting the *ancien regime* of unipolarity.

The Unipolar Imaginary

As suggested above, Carr teaches us that power conditions all our perspectives. Thus, all concepts, theories, and frameworks within IR need to be evaluated in light of unipolarity and the changing distribution of power in the international order. The first central claim of this book is, thus, that, just as Carr saw the liberal utopianism of the interbellum giving expression to a particular vision of US-inspired and Anglo-French world order, so too today the complex baroque superstructure of IR and its various crenellated battlements, flanking annexes, elaborate flying buttresses, and delicate spires are built on the foundations of the American-led world order. Unlike in Carr's day, when the international system was in the tortuous process of transitioning from a multipolar to a bipolar international system, we seem to be transitioning away from unipolar globalization to a new system.[45] All those seemingly solid walls of empirical findings and scientific mortar, right up to the shimmering spires of the most exquisite critical IR theories, need to be reassessed in light of these shaky foundations.

Analogously to Carr's critique, I argue that much of IR is utopian – expressing, however, the very particular utopianism of unipolarity. Heading up a special issue of the *European Journal of International Relations*, Tim Dunne, Lene Hansen, and Colin Wight asked in 2013 whether IR theory was coming to an end. They considered the evolution of the discipline through various forms, paradigms, paradigm wars, and supposed great debates, paying only limited attention however to how these intellectual contortions might reflect and intersect with changing patterns of political order (mainly with respect to the development of new weapons systems.)[46] Along similar lines, in the same journal David Lake welcomed the end of grand theory and great debates in preference for mid-range theory, such as the theory of democratic peace, concerning the allegedly pacific interactions of democratic states.[47] Why bother with devising grand claims about changing patterns of international order when the world was safely bundled up under the reign of a single superpower? Yet it is precisely mid-range theory that becomes far less tenable when a structural reconfiguration of international order is underway. It seems that grander theories are once again merited, as our given questions, assumptions, and frameworks can no longer be taken for granted.

Thus various pronouncements concerning the "end of IR," or invoking a "post-human IR" or criticising "anthropocenic IR" need to be seen for what they are: the conceits of unipolarity richly decorated with utopian flourishes – not least the belief that the petty squabbles of mankind, of jealous sovereigns and egotistical nations, have been transcended by the looming prospect of ecological collapse as a result of resource depletion and global warming. The political preconditions for this belief were quite clearly a highly integrated global capitalism and overweening US power, and were reflected in the impulses towards disciplinary expansion and annexation: "International Relations," Cameron Harrington grandly declared, "is no longer simply a sub-discipline of political science and economics, but also of the geophysical sciences."[48] It seems that it is easier to imagine a new geological era in the planet's history than to imagine even a relatively minor recalibration in the global balance of power in favour of China.

One of the grandest utopian flourishes is that of anthropocenic planetary politics. Anthony Burke and his collaborators drew up a manifesto for "Planet Politics" in 2016 that they hoped would supersede IR with a new global political project: "to end human-caused extinctions, prevent ... climate change, save the oceans, support vulnerable multi-species populations" and of course support "social justice," although the latter merely human-focused goal is predictably relegated to the end of the series.[49] The quasi-mystical invocation of integrated systems sustained by intricate webs of connection in which everything – "animals, microbes, devices, materials"[50] – is interconnected in a single, self-contained complex and in which even distinctions "between living and non-living objects and beings" is swallowed up – is nothing more than a series of glosses on unipolarity.[51] Critical theorists have long enjoyed ethical agonising over how far they are entitled to speak on behalf of the oppressed – even the doyenne of post-colonial theory, Gayatri Spivak, was alert to this pathology.[52] Yet this intellectual brooding is one means of assuaging guilt over critical theorists' own political impotence.

In IR, these dilemmas are typically resolved by finding ever more powerless, vulnerable, and marginalized groups to speak for: beleaguered ethnic minorities, impotent rebellions such as the Zapatistas, displaced refugees, landless peasants, the indigenous tribespeople of the Amazon. In speaking on behalf of "earth systems," critical theorists have found the perfect political subjects – or, in their parlance, "actants" – who have the advantage that they cannot speak for themselves but still need their mysteries to be interpreted by a specialised caste of latter-day soothsayers.[53] This is what we might call the green version of the unipolar imaginary, in which ecosystems and human governance systems blend into one mysterious unit. Yet the rights of dolphins in Batavia Bay or "crimes against biodiversity" could only ever be proffered as a political priority in a unipolar international system. Under current geopolitical conditions, establishing a new "Earth Systems Council," as urged by Burke and his collaborators, in which the Amazon Basin, the Arctic, Antarctic, and the Pacific Ocean would all enjoy the status of "nations," would not only necessitate neocolonialism in South America on a truly epic scale but would also be merely to grant extra votes to the US in international fora. These extra votes would in turn be used to squash Chinese industry while invoking the good of the planet.[54] This is the reality of geopolitics: increased power political competition will expose the limited, partial, and ideological character of global claims much more thoroughly and effectively than critical IR ever could or will.

Carr noted that expansionist, supranational political visions of universal integration recur throughout history – from the Eighteenth Dynasty of Ancient Egypt, across the Roman Empire through to China's Han Empire, to the medieval Catholic Church, to eighteenth-century French hegemony in Europe.[55] The "collapse of the biosphere" that bewitches the theorists of the Anthropocene will turn out to be the collapse of the unipolar world refracted through concepts that have become unmoored from the merely profane world of human politics. Indeed, as unipolarity fades, perhaps what we are confronting for the first time in modernity is genuinely *inter*-national relations that have decisively shifted beyond the Euro-Atlantic system. Against what Burke and his colleagues are arguing, we are returning to, rather than shifting away from, the "managed anarchy of nation-states." The "collective human interaction with the biosphere" that they envisage as the next stage of international politics is merely the utopian dream of the receding era of unipolarity.[56] The spectacular economic transformation that we have seen in China and (on current projections) that we will see in India later this century, means that our post-colonial international society will no longer simply be a flimsy superstructure of "quasi-states" crumbled over a world economy that is still largely Euro-American and the majority of whose members were descendants of the original signatories of the Westphalian treaties, but rather a genuinely internationalized world – a world, and not just two continents, of politically self-sufficient nations. Planet politics indeed.

In making the case for anthropocenic politics, Harrington argues in the journal *Millennium* that IR must be forced "into an uncomfortable place" by being wrenched "away from its natural habitat of the struggle for power and peace" to consider instead "the enmeshing of natural and social processes."[57] In fact, it is precisely the struggle for power and peace that is "the uncomfortable place" for IR. It is precisely this place – the "struggle for power and peace" – from which IR scholars have persistently sought refuge in various utopian schemes, whether theoretical or institutional – complex interdependence, supranationalism, globalization, international law, the League of Nations, the European Union and, more recently, wallowing in the cloying melancholia of eco-collapse – what we might term disaster utopianism. Meditating on "geopolitics at the end of the world," US critical theorist Jairus Victor Grove advocates a "pessimistic understanding of global politics" that could help "explain how we could come to a place where there is a sense of relief in watching everything come to an end."[58] That the end of US unipolarity could be confused with the end of the world only shows how deeply attached critical theorists are to US power. Tellingly, when Grove says that we now "own" the planet because we "broke" it, he is invoking a piece of American folk wisdom called the "Pottery Barn" rule, which was in turn popularised by US defence secretary Colin Powell, who justified US nation-building in Iraq on the grounds that it was the US that "broke" Iraq by invading it![59] What better illustration that the chimera of Anthropecenic politics could only emerge in a unipolar world? Grove offers up his cosmological pessimism as an antidote to "indifferentism and nihilism in the sense of the phenomenon of Donald Trump."[60] That Hillary Clinton's failure to take the White House in 2016 could be confused with the end of the world betokens the provincialism of a quintessentially Euro-American discipline. A more multipolar world fragmented by new geopolitical rivalries will be both simpler and less comfortable, and these various supra-political theories of international relations will be politicized once again. Instead of the grand declamations of transnational bureaucracies underpinned by US power, climate change in international politics will become a matter of changing patterns of industrialization, the opening up of new sea lanes and trade routes, commercial rivalry and geopolitical competition over rare earth minerals and new energy sources such as lithium, the resources of the deep sea bed, the warming Arctic, and in due course deeper into this century, perhaps even the competitive colonization of the melted polar icecaps, as these hitherto barren regions finally become accessible to mass human settlement.[61]

Critical Utopianism

Thus we see that that the discipline of IR, and particularly its most radical and critical variants, are but "unconscious reflexions of national policy based on a particular interpretation of the national interest at a particular time" – except that, unlike Carr's multipolar era, in which makeshift "collective interests" had to be invoked to blot out the reality of competing interests, our particular time is that of unipolar globalization in decline.[62] Thus the claim here is that many IR theories, and especially critical IR theories, are far more likely to express underlying relations of power than they are able to understand them, let alone critique them. That the disciplinary status of Critical IR has changed in recent years has not been lost on some critical scholars. Cynthia Weber likened this to a process of gentrification, in which critical theory has grown to constitute an "edgy neighbourhood" within the larger metropolis of disciplinary orthodoxy and convention: "a kind of East Village of multiple, interdisciplinary-mixed IRs whose residents have relatives in ... other disciplinary neighbourhoods."[63] What this felicitous if somewhat US-centric metaphor omits is that, aside from never being as edgy as promised, these districts exist in every major urban centre on the planet because the process of urban hipsterization has coincided with the financialization of the global economy, and it is this last change that has led to the corresponding transformation of urban cores. That is, the edgy urban enclaves were just another product of – and not a hold-out against – neoliberal financialization. So too with Critical IR: it is an organic by-product of unipolar globalization, not a besieged hold-out against it.

Anyone who bothers to step outside the edgy enclave will clearly see that, just as the hipsters have globalized, so too Critical IR is hegemonic, not peripheral, in the British academy today, and its intellectual empire sprawls far afield, encompassing both the Australasian and Canadian academies along with colonial offshoots embedded in the US as well as exerting a powerful pull over the Scandinavian academy.[64] This is the Critical Anglosphere – quite fittingly, an intellectual penumbra that maps fairly well onto the old actual Anglosphere.[65] As Carr observed so many years ago, "The study of international relations in English-speaking countries is simply a study of the best way to run the world from positions of strength."[66] This is as true now as it was back then, even if the content and character of that study may have changed in the interim.[67] The crypto-utopianism of Critical IR means that it is, like liberalism, a buttress of the political status quo, not least in its pervasive pedagogic influence, as we shall see in subsequent chapters. As there is already a growing critique of liberal hegemony in American IR, in this book I will mainly focus my fire on British / Critical IR with occasional side swipes at liberalism in general.

How then did the discipline of IR become so blithe and self-assured? The answer lies partly in the way in which knowledge in the discipline is constructed. This imperial system of knowledge is maintained by the most cunning form of orthodoxy and intellectual hegemony yet devised – orthodoxy that masquerades as heterodoxy, an orthodoxy dedicated to perpetual insurgency in which the "core" is hollowed out but never overthrown or replaced. I was initially surprised as a graduate student to sit through plenary sessions, keynote lectures, and round-tables and see highly paid, well-respected research professors proclaim how marginalized they were within the academy, and how they represented dissident forms of suppressed, exotic knowledges.[68] I came to realise that this tactic not only obviates the need for disciplinary leadership or consensus – let alone progress – it also ensures that intellectual challenge is impossible, as any criticism of the new hegemony can be pre-emptively cast as intellectual privilege and politically motivated efforts at suppression, thus making for bad faith rather than intellectual engagement or substantive critique. As observed by Paul Cammack in a wonderful paper on the derelictions of critical international political economy, it is an intellectual field "shaped by gate-keeping and the pursuit of [academic] power and empire."[69] The same is true of Critical IR more broadly.

Part of this refusal to claim intellectual authority was maintained by re-enacting the ritual slaughter of theoretical realism for the benefit of incoming undergraduates and postgraduates. The claim to intellectual marginalization is frequently maintained by arguing in "IR 101" that realism is a pernicious, still-dominant, and domineering ideology of militaristic nationalism and state conceit. Realists, suitably cowed, have responded in turn by draining realism of its "dangerous" elements, such as political interests and state power – a theme we shall return to in the conclusion of this book.[70] We have seen that Critical IR has on the whole been complicit in the era of permanent war brought about under liberal hegemony, and that this has helped them evade the task of self-criticism. As should be evident, this reflects how far Critical IR is also conditioned by power. This last point was driven home to me while observing a roundtable of critical luminaries at a convention of the European International Studies Association in Barcelona in September 2017, only weeks before the referendum on Catalan independence was held in that city despite being banned by the central government in Madrid, and which was (predictably) not even mentioned during the discussion. When one commentator from the audience asked how the panellists could so blithely ignore major political events such as the sabre-rattling of the Trump administration towards North Korea and the possibility of nuclear war, a member of the panel confidently swatted this aside, saying that the stand-off over the Korean peninsula was of little consequence as the US joint chiefs of staff could be relied upon to constrain any rash behaviour by the president. In other words, the US deep state could be relied upon to constrain a democratically elected national leader in order to ensure that the world could be kept safe for knowingly oblivious critical theorizing. Rarely in my career have I seen the contempt for democracy, the tacit complicity with existing power structures, and the casual indifference not only to the local politics of the conference venue but also to world politics at large so condensed in a single moment – and at a conference on world politics no less.

As a rule of thumb, it could be said that the more self-avowedly critical the theory, the less critical of power it actually is. One hundred years after the discipline was founded, the leading "spirits of our age" took "out of the mass of current speculation" precisely "that body of theory which corresponded to their needs, consciously and unconsciously fitting their practice to it, and it to their practice"[71] – in this case, starting from liberal and constructivist theorising and fanning out across the many variants of critical approaches. As we have already seen, self-avowedly "reflectivist" and critical schools of thought become unwitting exponents of global hierarchies of power, and this should alert us to the weaknesses within the structures of these theories themselves. These weaknesses are the subject matter of chapter 2 in particular. As these theories and frameworks are but "unconscious reflexions" of existing power structures, these same theories, concepts, and ideas will diminish by the same proportion as Western power diminishes. As the liberal international order enters crisis, so too these theories become ever more confounded and confusing. Given that all these critical theories express the era of unipolarity, an international system dominated by a single overwhelmingly powerful state, as that margin of power is eroded, the parochialism, one-sidedness, and ornamental character of these IR theories will also be increasingly exposed.

Yet, as has already been intimated, our utopianism is different, as is the character of the international system. Carr castigated the utopians of his day for their rigid attachment to the status quo and a flawed victor's peace. No such accusation could be levelled at the utopians of today, who have actively supported the transformation of the status quo through democratization, liberalization, defending human rights by force if necessary – the era of liberal hegemony has been more a red-dimmed utopianism of war than a feeble-minded utopia of law and peace. Similarly, while Carr could only cite long-dead political theorists in support of realism in his day, today realism is still a vital strain of IR theorizing, even enjoying a new bloom of health in the form of the attempt to renew classical realism (albeit drawing more heavily on the German-American Hans J. Morgenthau than Carr).

Carr envisaged the practice of political science as a teetering balance that oscillated in perpetuity between these two extremes, utopianism outweighing realism in his own day.[72] Yet this problematic image of balance leaves us condemned to live between these oscillations, as the beam that holds up the pans freighted with realism on one side and utopianism on the other will constantly waver back and forth. Any actual equilibrium between the two will almost certainly be tremulous, rare and fleeting. Even less propitiously, John J. Mearsheimer cast the disciplinary divide in IR as a perpetual war between the forces of realism on the one side and the massed ranks of idealism on the other – an image he promoted in the E.H. Carr Memorial Lecture that he delivered in Carr's alma mater, the University of Wales at Aberystwyth, on 14 October 2004.[73] Although Mearsheimer left a predictably impressive trail of intellectual destruction in the course of this foray into the enemy camp of British IR, he nonetheless failed to specify how British IR embodies what Carr saw as utopianism. He also (unlike Carr) fails to reckon with how the terrain on which the battle is fought itself has changed – not least in the fact that Critical IR is an expression of a distinctive type of unipolar political order. Thus our task of critique will require more than Carr's attempt at mere intellectual equilibration, or simply joining battle in Mearsheimer's intellectual Forever War.

Carr also held that the utopian impulses of interwar IR represented an infantile disorder, a malady of youthful exuberance in a discipline that was at the time only two decades old. Carr hoped that realism would yield political maturity, sobriety and wisdom, even if only temporarily. Unfortunately, well past its hundredth year, no such grace and clemency could be extended to our discipline at this stage. Its maladies are clearly those of senescence rather than youthful ebullience. As we confront the crumbling of our own liberal international order a hundred years after the founding of the discipline and eighty years after the publication of Carr's text, the stakes are high as to whether we are capable of escaping Carr's dialectic of utopianism and realism. A stock-taking and ruthless reordering is well overdue. Carr conceived of his book as a counter-hegemonic assault on the hegemony of liberal rationalism and utopianism; so too this book is conceived as a counter-hegemonic critique of Critical IR.[74] How far it succeeds is for the reader to judge; however, before we consider what that might involve, a brief note of clarification.

This is emphatically *not* a book of "Carr Studies."[75] There is a complex and sophisticated discussion in IR surrounding Carr and his evolving views of international affairs across the first half of the twentieth century. As Keith Smith observes, "Where once textbook caricatures littered the landscape, the subtleties and nuances of Carr's international thought now dominate, and quite rightfully so."[76] I would hazard however that we may have gone too far in the opposite direction, and that over-growth in an increasingly scholastic "Carr Studies" risks obscuring the trunk of his work, which poses to us the harder and more important question – how far do Carr's ideas still enable us to actually grasp international politics today?[77] If this book offers anything to debates around Carr so much the better, but it is less a study of Carr than an attempt to apply Carr: to sharpen and reuse his "theoretical weapons" to help us slice apart the interlocking structures of ideas, institutions, theories and practices that have dominated world politics over the last two decades. It is also determinedly addressed to our contemporary era and its challenges and, as already suggested above, I will seek to think with Carr to go past him as, from our historical vantage point, his limitations are just as stimulating and intriguing as his insights.

In what follows, the first chapter undertakes a critical comparison of Carr's twenty years' crisis – what we might term the "classical interbellum" of international politics, the period 1919–1939 – and our own twenty years' crisis, the era from 1999 to 2019. Drawing on Carr's classic account of this period, *The Twenty Years' Crisis*, as well as some of his other books published during this era, I compare how far his framework still applies to our own era. I also justify why we should date the start of our crisis to 1999 and why a cycle of crisis appeared to have come to a close by the end of 2019. The next chapter considers new forms of utopianism in international affairs today. Given that "liberal hegemony" is coming under fire in the recent critiques provided by John J. Mearsheimer and Stephen M. Walt, instead of repeating or glossing their arguments against liberal hegemony (or indeed repeating arguments I have made elsewhere about certain aspects of contemporary international liberalism), I consider critical theory and constructivism instead. Both of these theories present themselves in pointed contrast to ideals of liberal hegemony as well as political realism, so seeing how they become affirmative of the status quo is the purpose of chapter 2. I show that their failure to consider basic questions of politics and power mean that both of these theoretical frameworks have become utopian in Carr's sense, which is to say aspirational and normative rather than scientific or critical, and thereby moulded to fit the needs of power today. In particular, I show how constructivist theorists, insistent on the fundamental malleability of all social and political life, have effectively recreated the notion of the harmony of interests that was scorned by Carr, and thus they too have tended to obfuscate the reality of political power and clashes over it. As constructivists prioritise identity over interests, their notion that it was possible to transform interests by transforming identities prompted the recreation of the old liberal utopianism – that all political conflict will be resolved through the convergence of interests, after everyone has been harmonised in a new thickly woven international society of virtuous businesses, enlightened non-governmental organizations, transnational agencies and benevolent supranational authorities. That this vision happened to coincide with a new peak in US power was, of course, entirely accidental. I also show that critical theorists have slouched into a convoluted liberalism that evades questions of state power and political interests through their emphasis on global social movements.

The third chapter takes aim at that institution that most clearly embodies utopianism in the international order today – the European Union, that continent-spanning political order in which the intertwining of liberal utopian theories and politics has been so destructive and irrational. Here I make the argument that Eutopians have effectively vindicated Carr by reversing the historical sequence described by Carr in his *Twenty Years' Crisis*. Whereas Carr saw nineteenth-century liberalism as impossible to sustain in the face of the massification of politics seen in the twentieth century, Eutopians have quite literally constructed a supranational harmony of interests by de-massifying politics at the continental level as European elites retreated into the star chambers of Brussels. The EU proves the validity of Carr's view that the harmony of interests is incompatible with mass politics, but in reverse. For the EU involves constantly constructing a harmony of intra-European elite interests. This time however they are legitimated not by warmed over eighteenth-century liberalism, but rather sophisticated (and sometimes not so sophisticated) – but no less utopian – theories of European integration. Thus transnational integration is rooted in the hollowing out of national political systems and is therefore built on fragile foundations: once again, the liberal utopian project will fall to the incursions of mass politics. All this said (and as already indicated), Carr is not an unfailing theoretical lodestone either. The final chapter thus seeks to move beyond Carr himself, making the case for the need to escape the intellectual framework of the twenty years' crisis, itself a reified artefact of twentieth-century international order.

1 Carr's Crisis and Ours, 1919–1939/1999–2019

We ask ourselves, over and over, "Is the liberal international order crumbling?" Yet we have been here before. Over eighty years ago, Carr stood on the precipice of a crumbling international order in circumstances that were far graver than ours. He was clear that the answer was "yes." By the time *The Twenty Years' Crisis* was published in July 1939, conscription had already been operating in Britain for two months. Fascism was on the march not through the "normalisation" of its discourse but through force of arms. Only a few months earlier, the last citadel of Republican Spain, Barcelona, had fallen to General Franco's rebel forces, thereby ending the Spanish Civil War. Italian dictator Benito Mussolini had annexed Albania, snuffing out the independence of a state less than three decades old. That came shortly after Hitler had annexed and dismembered the rump of the Czecho-Slovak state, following his annexation of the Sudetenland the year before. All of this was only within Europe. A few years earlier, Mussolini had extinguished the last independent African state when Abyssinia was annexed to the Italian empire in 1936. From the prospective vantage point of our Asian Century, one could also plausibly say that the Second World War had already broken out two years before the publication of Carr's book, in July 1937, with the eruption of fully fledged war between China and Japan, over two years before Hitler's invasion of Poland.[1] In any case, before the end of 1939, Hitler and Stalin would invade Poland, precipitating war with Britain and France, and Stalin's Soviet Union would invade Finland.

In light of the problems confronting Carr when he was writing, we might be tempted to adopt that old Viennese saw, "The situation is grave, but not serious" when considering our own problems. Yet if this ironic, fin-de-siècle quip is apposite to our situation, then things may indeed get a lot more serious, as of course they did in 1914 when the oncoming Great War would sweep away the senile and decadent cosmopolitan order embodied in the Austro-Hungarian Empire. Despite the apparently monumental scale of these challenges, when analysing them in the *Twenty Years' Crisis* at least, Carr adopted a tone of relative equanimity, if not indeed relief. The end of the crisis represented the sweeping away of the liberal international order, a Procrustean framework of naive nineteenth-century and American expectations that simply could no longer contain new economic and political realities, as embodied in the military insurgency of those Carr described as the "have not" nations – the Axis powers. No one stands in Carr's position today. Even those who do not think the liberal international order is about to be swept away are far from optimistic: G.J. Ikenberry thinks the liberal international order will survive by default, simply due to the absence of challengers; Beate Jahn argues that it will require recalibrating the relationship between domestic and international order.[2] Is anything to be learned from Carr's equanimity in confronting the disintegration of an entire world order?

When was Liberalism?

In many ways, the liberal international order of the inter-war period – the interbellum – remains the archetype of liberal order *tout court* – and this not least a result of Carr's own critique and the mythos of a "founding great debate" that established the classical bifurcation in approaching world order – namely, realism and liberalism. All the basic tropes of international politics are there, tightly compacted into the twenty years of the interbellum: aggressive nationalist expansionism, territorial irredentism, a new balance of power, spiralling arms races, small-scale ethnic rivalries interlocking with large-scale geopolitical rivalry, heavy transnational debts and economic ruin, failed post-war reconstruction, flawed peace settlements, crowned by a failed international organisation, the League of Nations. Indeed it is remarkable – as we shall see in greater detail below – just how much our contemporary politics is *still* organised around themes inherited from the interbellum – anti-fascism, the horror of appeasement and concomitant readiness for pre-emptive action, and how haunted we are still by the failure and disintegration of the League of Nations. "We created a United Nations Security Council," US President George W. Bush told the UN General Assembly in September 2002, while making the case for war in Iraq, "so that, unlike the League of Nations, our deliberations would be more than talk, our resolutions would be more than wishes."[3] Indeed, our contemporary order is built on the ruined foundations of the interbellum – constitutionally and structurally, our United Nations is remarkably similar to the League that was so despised by Carr. Yet despite the fact that the post-war 1945 world has endured nearly four times as long as the interwar period and withstood even the dangers of nuclear war, it seems that we still cannot shake the feeling that we live in an interregnum between world wars.

In the stylised story so frequently told of the discipline of IR, international liberalism is usually backdated to 1919 and the presidency of Woodrow Wilson, who put into motion ideas stemming from an earlier period that could be tracked back to the late-eighteenth-century philosophy of Immanuel Kant.[4] It is a narrative of an oddly teleological bent, as it is set up to fail – Woodrow Wilson here cast as the ingenuous and optimistic dreamer, whose visions of peace and democracy were doomed to be dashed against the rocky outcrops of power politics and ruthless totalitarianism. There are many aspects of this stylised narrative, still so prevalent in textbooks, which could reasonably be questioned. Not least of these is the image of Woodrow Wilson as the benevolent but naive idealist, instead of what he was – a ruthless politician fanatically committed to racial hierarchy as well as to crushing political dissent at home while extensively deploying military force abroad.[5] Quite aside from historical realities such as these, what is odd about it is how its teleological cast of liberal failure and realist correction supplied by the likes of Carr and Hans J. Morgenthau paradoxically lays the ground for a renewed liberal international order, embodied in the post-war United Nations and its Charter framework.

Yet if we take the League of Nations to embody "liberalism 1.0" and assume that the liberalism 2.0 that was uploaded in 1945 was upgraded to incorporate the likes of Carr's criticisms, Carr was clear that even liberalism 1.0 was already obsolete.[6] In Carr's view, liberalism had already reached its acme under the British Empire in the nineteenth century, and it was now artificially prolonged and extruded back into Europe by Wilson, from an America that had only by accident of its geography escaped the reality of geopolitical competition, and, by virtue of its vantage point of isolation, wealth, and power, misconceived the fundamentals of international politics. Indeed, had he been familiar with the term, perhaps Carr might have been tempted to call liberalism 1.0 "zombie liberalism." Strikingly – and it is a theme we shall return to – it is the liberal idealists and *not* the Soviets or fascists whom Carr castigated as being deluded. Indeed, inasmuch as ideology enters Carr's discussion it is to criticise liberals, and it was the liberals whom Carr saw as not only naive but positively dangerous in their efforts to fit the fluidity of European power politics into obsolete political notions and rigid legal frameworks.

Liberalism could reasonably be traced back to the Dutch Revolt of the 1568–1648 Eighty Years' War, in which the United Provinces emerged from Habsburg absolutism. Certainly by the time of the 1756–63 Seven Years' War – the first global war with transcontinental battlefields – the British were claiming to defend liberty against French absolutism, and the Enlightenment philosopher David Hume was suggesting that an international balance of power was necessary to preserve liberty.[7] In other words, liberalism was indeed old by the interbellum of the twentieth century, whereas from the textbooks and lecture halls of the early twenty-first century liberalism is presented as being in the first bloom of youth. By the inter-war period, the decrepitude of liberal internationalism was evident in the greater, more concentrated and institutionalised efforts needed to coordinate and police international order – what Inis L. Claude, Jr. called the "organising tendency" of international politics that was displacing the vision of a decentralised global civil society or "empire of liberty," coordinated by the Bank of England, the Royal Navy, and the gold standard, as in the nineteenth century.[8]

Carr's claim about liberal utopianism being artificially prolonged past the nineteenth century is at once highly insightful and at the same time deeply ambivalent and contradictory. On the one hand, we do need reminding of Carr's claim with respect to modern international history, especially given that as far as the discipline of IR is concerned liberalism is so often assumed to begin in 1919, or at best, following (liberal) democratic peace theory, in 1815 following the Congress of Vienna (ironically, the moment when the Holy Alliance was seeking to crush liberalism). On the other hand, if Carr's insight into liberal senescence needs to be borne in mind, so too does the restoration of a liberal international order after 1945 – a restoration that would para-doxically be reinforced by the Soviet state through its half-hearted support for Third World decolonisation, thereby cutting against the territorial agglomeration which Carr took the USSR to embody. In a period in which the challenges to liberal internationalism were much, much greater than our own and in which Carr looked forward to a new dispensation of vast, self-sufficient regional power-blocs rather than a plurality of nation-states (indeed, he did not shy away from adopt-ing the Nazis' favoured concept of *Grossraum*), a new liberal order was born, albeit one that embedded great power privileges in the global su-premacy of the veto-wielding, permanent members of the UN Security Council. In an era in which the challenges to liberal international order are nowhere near as severe, we should be cautious before too quickly intoning the last rites over the corpse of liberal internationalism, nor indeed imagine that its potential replacements are better. All of this is by way of saying that a comparison of Carr's crisis and ours should be an effective way of examining context and precedent for our contem-porary travails.

Distant Mirror

As should be clear, rereading Carr's account of the interbellum is an eerie exercise – not only his *Twenty Years' Crisis* but also its more em-pirically based precursor originally published in 1937, *International Relations between the Two World Wars*.[9] There are many points, remarks, observations and analyses – indeed some made *en passant* – that could have been written to describe our own era, not only in international politics but also international economics. For a time in which Europe was still at the core of world politics, Carr's perspective is strikingly global.[10] He notes, for example, the challenge posed by economic development in India and China in undermining the industrial supremacy of the Western advanced economies.[11] From the vantage point of our era of rapid Asian economic growth, it is the Sino-Indian autarky of the Cold War that seems the peculiar interregnum, while Asian industrial dynamism fits the pre-Cold War pattern better. Carr also draws attention to the recurrence of anti-Semitism in Europe as a hallmark of political tensions and economic stress, as well as the agitation in Britain against "unrestricted alien immigration." He notes how across the Western world, "in place of the natural flow of migration came the problem of forcibly evicted refugees" – words that echo with the Syrian refugee crisis since 2011.[12] Carr was particularly attuned to the changing response to refugees as a gauge with which to measure the collapse of international liberalism.[13] His cursory dismissal of the "Green Book of Abyssinian Atrocities," compiled by the Italians to justify the invasion of Abyssinia in 1935, could bring to mind any number of humanitarian claims made for the "crusading rights of civilization" in our own time.[14]

Carr's invocation of the colonial theorist Lord Lugard's critique of international administration could almost be written for our own interminable debates on UN peacebuilding operations, which also pose the risk of paralysing "all initiative by the dead hand of a super-bureaucracy devoid of national sentiment and stifling to all patriotism, [which] would be very disadvantageous to the countries concerned."[15] Carr's observation that "Power is indivisible; and the military and economic weapons are merely different instruments of power" could have been written of the Eurozone today.[16] Carr's description of interlocking structures of markets and political influence across Central Europe could equally apply to Central Europe today if one were to map the pattern of German industrial investment across Poland, Hungary, the Czech Republic and Slovakia[17] – or as Carr pithily summarised – "Germany reconstituted *Mittel-Europa* and pressed forward into the Balkans."[18] Writing in the aftermath of the Great Depression, Carr's observation that "Purchasing power had become an international asset" could apply to US strategy in the trade wars of our day, as the Trump administration has sought to erode the trade surpluses accumulated by both China and Germany.[19] Carr's sneering at the delusions that accompanied interwar British decline could have been written as a critique of theorists of the so-called Anglosphere eighty years *avant la lettre*, still dreaming of "CANZUK" – Canada, Australia, New Zealand, UK, or the white Commonwealth 2.0 – so many years after Carr penned these lines:

> Most contemporary Englishmen are aware that the conditions which secured the overwhelming ascendancy of Great Britain in the nineteenth century no longer exist. But they sometimes console themselves with the dream that British supremacy, instead of passing altogether away, will be transmuted into the higher and more effective form of an ascendancy of the English-speaking peoples. The *pax Britannica* will ... become a *pax Anglo-Saxonica*, under which the British Dominions ... will be cunningly woven into a fabric of Anglo-American co-operation.[20]

Carr's perspicacity extended beyond the *Twenty Years' Crisis* too. In his wartime editorials for the *Times*, while he decried the "German Dream" of a "Europe united by conquest" he noted that any alternative European order "cannot be achieved [except] through cooperation"[21] – a conclusion that could apply just as well to the Eurozone today. Carr's critique of British foreign policy in the early days of the Cold War and his advice to face inwards rather than outwards could also have been written for Britain today, emerging from the EU and buffeted between the neo-imperialists pining for the Commonwealth on the one hand, and the Euro-imperialists horrified by Britain's attempt to exercise its sovereignty on the other:

> It may be that the question whether war breaks out between Russia and America affects us far more than the question whether we can increase the productivity of labour or improve the organization of industry or the distribution of consumer goods. But the point is that we can do hardly anything about the first question and a great deal about the second.[22]

With analysis such as this, Stefan Collini's designation of Carr as the "historian of the future" would still seem apt. Carr's contempt for British cultural pessimism, which he attributed to intellectuals and not the "man in the street," was to him indicative of "a form of elitism, a yearning for lost privilege" – something that is all too apparent today in the yearning of the British intelligentsia for the lost world of May 2016 before the shock of the Brexit vote in June that year.[23] Carr noted that in "a limited number of countries, nineteenth-century liberal democracy had been a brilliant success. It was a success because its presuppositions coincided with the stage of development reached by the countries concerned." The liberal democracies "scattered throughout the world by the peace settlement of 1919 ... the product of abstract theory, stuck no roots in the soil, and quickly shrivelled away."[24] Here, we need only think of the current governments of Hungary, Poland, Slovakia, Macedonia, Montenegro and Serbia to see a failure once again to consolidate liberal democracy across Central and Eastern Europe and the Balkans, although the fault today is that of the EU and not Woodrow Wilson. The resilience of authoritarian global powers such as China and Russia, and regional hegemons such as Turkey, Iran and Saudi Arabia, all reinforce the limited reach of liberal democracy in the aftermath of our twenty-year crisis.

Carr's summary of the international order in 1939 is worth quoting at length:

> What confronts us in international politics today is, therefore, nothing less than the complete bankruptcy of the conception of morality which has dominated political and economic thought for a century and a half. Internationally, it is no longer possible to deduce virtue from right reasoning, because it is no longer seriously possible to believe that every state, by pursuing the greatest good of the whole world, is pursuing the greatest good of its own citizens, and *vice versa*. The synthesis of morality and reason, at any rate in the crude form in which it was achieved by nineteenth-century liberalism, is untenable. The inner meaning of the modern international crisis is the collapse of the whole structure of utopianism based on the harmony of interests. The present generation will need to rebuild from the foundations.[25]

Swap "thirty years" for a "century and a half," and "twenty-first" for "nineteenth-century liberalism," and everything Carr says here applies today. The question posed for us too then is, can we once again rebuild from the foundations up?

Yet, at the same time we know that many things are very self-evidently different. Albania was restored to Italy's sphere of influence since the Italian military intervention in that country, Operation Alba, in 1997. Italy also invoked the crusading rights of civilization 2.0 – the so-called responsibility to protect – in justifying its military assault on its former colony Libya, in 2011. Yet these military operations were both authorised and coordinated as multinational endeavours, and while EU political interference in Libya has clear neocolonial overtones, the fact remains that neither Albania nor Libya will be incorporated into a new Italian empire. This new Italian sphere of influence, such as it is, is not only sublimated into EU neocolonialism but is also much reduced when compared to the Italian empire of the interbellum, not least because it no longer extends down to the Horn of Africa. Ethiopia, on the other hand, while still authoritarian, nonetheless remains definitively republican and independent and is one of Africa's fastest growing and most dynamic economies.[26] Last but by no means least, Italy is not a fascist dictatorship, and while it may indeed be a "have not" power in the context of the Eurozone, its grievances are not expressed through territorial irredentism.

The differences do not stop there; it is very clearly a different world in many other respects. In light of how Brexit negotiations have been pursued, few could share Carr's supremely confident respect for the British civil service.[27] In the *Twenty Years' Crisis* Carr discusses British policy in Egypt and Palestine, yet today Britain dominates neither and its influence in both places is significantly less than that of other states. Whereas Germany may well have a new sphere of economic influence in Southeastern Europe and even further afield (as indeed Carr had urged back in the interbellum), the sterling bloc, against which Germany was erecting its own zone of exclusive economic privileges, is long gone. Whereas Carr could reasonably consider in 1939 what role Britain might play in Chinese post-war reconstruction, British capital has little if any significance for the long-term growth of Chinese industry today. Indeed, the opposite may be true. British defence minister Gavin Williams's pathetic attempt to flaunt British military prowess by sending a warship to the South China Sea in early 2018 demonstrates the immaturity of Britain's ruling elite when confronted with the growth of Chinese economic power. French influence in Europe is no longer wielded through French investments across Eastern Europe, and, more amusingly, Carr's confident expectation that the "abolition or restriction of industrial profits" was self-evidently the wave of the future is also clearly not the case.[28] Other observations Carr made elsewhere seem no less naive in retrospect, sometimes even touchingly so, as when he claimed that "the American constitution has up to the present virtually precluded the assumption by the United States of an obligation to make war in any circumstances whatsoever."[29]

When is the Crisis?

Anniversary dates aside, questions of comparison invite questions of dates. Punctuated by two global wars involving all the major powers of the day, the interbellum could self-evidently be seen as a single compacted crisis. Yet Eric Hobsbawm mused whether "Thirty Years' War" would be a better designation for the interbellum, with continuous violence stretching across the period between the two world wars and arising out of interlocking and ideologically inflected civil and international wars for which the (First) Thirty Years' War of 1618–48 was the only precedent. Questions of the interbellum also raise questions of the larger frames into which we embed our twenty years' crisis. Hobsbawm famously dated a short twentieth century around the fate of the Russian Revolution, from 1914 to 1991, ending the "long nineteenth century" that he stretched from 1789 to 1914. Adam Tooze suggests an alternative framing around the twentieth century rise and fall of American power, from 1917, with Woodrow Wilson's entry into the First World War, through to 2016 with Trump's taking of the White House.

The label and concept of crisis itself seems to have taken on new meaning in recent times. At the time of writing, a Google n-gram will show how the word "crisis" explodes in frequency of use *in our own time*, only recently overreaching the previous peak of the 1930s! After all, the easiest way to elicit sympathy and responsiveness and to channel energy and resources to one's preferred sphere of attention is to declare a crisis, whether that be in education, in the family, in marriage, in universities, in child-rearing, in physics, in any number of economic sectors and industries, let alone in countries and regions. Perhaps indeed Carr himself contributed to this intellectual debasement of the concept by suggesting that "crisis" can be meaningfully stretched over decades. Others, such as Carr's contemporary Elizabeth Wiskemann, cast the politics of central Europe in terms of a "five hundred years crisis"![30] On an earlier anniversary of the publication of Carr's *Twenty Years' Crisis*, the editors of a scholarly collection of essays, Tim Dunne, Michael Cox and Ken Booth, went as far as to claim a continuous eighty years' crisis since 1919. They felt justified in doing so by citing the world war, civil wars, generalised violent upheaval, explosive innovation in military technology, decades of nuclear rivalry, collapsing economies and even "silent genocide of the poor and malnourished" as sufficient justification for this label.[31] These scholars brushed aside concerns that crisis itself necessitated a discrete, compact and self-contained period, arguing that the gravity and scale of these problems meant there was a ... crisis. In other words, the average life-span of a late-twentieth-century Westerner was entirely consumed with crisis. Ten years later, Michael Cox argued that the strains of the war on terror and the economic crash of 2008 motivated a return to Carr as an analyst of the crisis and limits of liberalism.[32]

Certainly carving out any twenty-year block of time out of the last eighty years since Carr's book was published would find sufficient drama, conflict and mighty challenges to constitute crisis, especially for those living through it. Take the twenty years since the end of the Second World War. That period saw the global spread of nuclear weapons to Soviet Russia, Britain, France and China, the Berlin Blockade in 1948, the consolidation of Cold War military blocs with NATO and the Warsaw Pact, the 1950–53 Korean War and the Cuban Missile Crisis in 1962. At the other end of the century, the twenty years from, say, 1985 to 2005, swept from the very peak of the second Cold War through the wonder and dread associated with the disintegration of the USSR, accompanied by palpable terror over the prospect of nuclear weapons falling into terrorists' hands, while Iraq was plunged into perpetual war by the West and global jihadism emerged. The exercise could probably be repeated for any twenty-year cycle in modern times: 1998–2008, 1958–78, 1964–84, 1973–93, etc., etc. Taking all this together, perhaps the most apposite response would be that of István Hont, and to resignedly describe modern international politics as embodying the "permanent crisis of a divided mankind."[33] By the same token, any number of grand human achievements could be plucked from these periods too, and offered as counterpoints to the tales of violent upheaval and disintegration. Not only were there a range of scientific, medical and technological breakthroughs, but many worse crises were indeed prevented – not least nuclear war between the superpowers.

Yet it was clear enough even at the time that 2016 represented a turning point for the international order, with the British vote to withdraw/secede from the EU and Donald Trump's electoral victory in the US, on a campaign platform that explicitly lambasted the institutions of liberal international order – that is, America's wars, America's alliance systems, America's international agreements and America's regional and global trading structures. In retrospect, there were several other events that year that were also of enduring importance – namely, the fall of Aleppo to Syrian government forces and Turkish president Recep Erdoğan's crushing of an attempted coup by a portion of his military forces. In the first case, the fall of Aleppo marked the turning of the tide in favour of the government in Syria's civil war. The fall of a nerve centre of the anti-government insurgency – an insurgency that had been lavished with enormous political and financial support by Western states and their regional allies – brought to an ignominious and bloody end the era of Western regime change operations. Syrian leader Bashar al-Assad would thus seemingly survive where Manuel Noriega, Slobodan Milošević, Saddam Hussein, Laurent Gbagbo, Muammar Gaddafi, and Viktor Yanukovych had all variously been ousted, exiled, killed, or hauled off to face the infinite reach of transnational justice. In Turkey, President Erdoğan rolled over from crushing mutinous military officers into a sweeping and brutal campaign to eliminate a spectrum of political opponents, thereby consolidating a new authoritarian regime.

Thus events in Syria and Turkey in 2016 could be taken as marking a symbolic end of Western policies of democratisation and regime change that had dominated the previous two decades. The last few years since have seen these dynamics of broad political change play out and carry us towards the end of President Trump's first term of office, with the presumptive appointment of the Brezhnev-like Joe Biden as Democratic presidential candidate at the time of writing a clear marker of American political decline. In the intervening period, we have seen both Turkish and Western humanitarian intervention in the Syrian civil war, the crumbling of the Iranian nuclear agreement, the US withdrawal from the Paris climate agreement, the Singapore and Hanoi summits between North Korea and the US, through to the election of hard right president Jair Bolsanaro in Brazil explicitly mimicking Trumpism, and the eruption of mass civil unrest in France in late 2018. By the end of 2019, the world itself had "taken to the streets" according to the *Economist*, with large anti-government protests having swept Algeria, Bolivia, Britain, Catalonia, Chile, the Czech Republic, Ecuador, France, Guinea, Haiti, Honduras, Hong Kong, Iraq, Iran, Kazakhstan, Lebanon, and Pakistan.[34] Then in late December reports emerged in China of the outbreak of a new corona virus. When might we usefully say this turbulence and change was set in motion?

When Carr draped the interbellum with the label "Twenty Years' Crisis," he did not mean to suggest a single block of unrelieved, solid political tension and insuperable challenges unleavened by any possibility for change and improvement. Rather it was to suggest that the very clear and immediate crisis of the late 1930s associated with Italian, German and Japanese expansionism stretched back to the flaws of the post-war settlement twenty years earlier. These flaws had in turn been perpetuated by the naive illusions of what Carr called utopianism, that were embodied in various political and legal structures that made the political system of the era evasive, rigid and unresponsive, thereby exacerbating the crisis. Analogously, I would argue that the roots of our current problems can be dated to 1999, thereby making it legitimate to conceptually interpret the problems of this period as being of a single piece.

There were a number of politically significant events in 1999 that set in motion processes that can be seen working themselves out over the course of the subsequent twenty years and carrying us through to the present. Here we can highlight some of the most important. The year 1999 was the year in which US military spending – still the greatest in the world at that point – began to grow again after having shrunk since the end of the Cold War. Notably, this started under a Democratic administration and occurred a full two years before the terror attacks of September 2001 that would precipitate a new round of US interventionism around the globe, including the aggressive export of liberalism. With growth in military spending briefly checked under the Obama administration following the 2008 crash, the Trump administration has continued to propel US military spending to ever greater heights.[35] The year 1999 also saw the US Senate refusing to ratify the Comprehensive Test Ban Treaty, thereby not only perpetuating a consistent pattern of US exemptionalism from international structures that is independent of the occupant of the White House, but also setting in motion the degradation of Cold War-era structures of nuclear deterrence that would, in turn, take us through to the renewed Russo-American nuclear rivalry of our era.

The year 1999 also saw the start of the Second Chechen War, and with it the substitution of a violent struggle for national self-determination with a murderous globalised jihadism in the Islamic world, as well as Vladimir Putin's consolidation of power as heir apparent to Russia's first post-Soviet leader, Boris Yeltsin. The year would end with Yeltsin's resignation in favour of Putin, marking the end of an era in which the West had sought to manage Russia as a supplicant client state. Putin's ascent to power would fortuitously coincide with a dramatic growth in the average price of crude oil after the historic lows of the previous fifteen years, thereby helping to buoy his regime and its capacity for self-assertion. Although the "liberal era" in Russian foreign policy had long since ended even under Yeltsin, the illusion that there were only positive sum gains in Russo-Western relations would prevail as long as Russia was economically prostrate. It was this historic, abiding boost to the price of oil that would allow Russian power to recuperate and that would eventually puncture the illusion that Western policy in Europe had transcended competitive geopolitics. Together with developments in the US, here were sown the seeds of new geopolitical rivalries.

More important, however, 1999 was also the year that saw the expansion of NATO eastwards to absorb former members of the Warsaw Pact, thereby violating the mutual East-West understanding developed at the end of the Cold War. The ultimate logic of this eastwards expansion would lead us to the war in Ukraine that we see today.[36] What was significant about NATO's absorption of the Višegrád states was that it was cast in the transcendent terms of European integration, was widely seen as a preamble to joining the EU and thus a providential consolidation of liberal democratic norms across the continent. This was liberal utopianism in the classical mould, drastically overestimating the legitimacy of supposedly universal values, oblivious to the fact that even the most exalted universalistic claims would inevitably be contaminated with power politics in the international arena, and forgetting that only those who have shaped an order have an active interest in maintaining it.[37] In short, the beginning of NATO expansion eastwards would inevitably be seen as menacing by Russia. As Kevork Oskanian has argued, the eastwards expansion of NATO readily fits the naive idealist paradigm criticised by Carr, and is even comprehensible in straightforward terms taken from Carr's analysis.[38]

The other significant aspect of our twenty years' crisis was the political evolution of the left, which has shifted a full 180 degrees over this period. From standing on the cusp of a globalised social revolt with the so-called Battle of Seattle in 1999 when demonstrators protested the meeting of the World Trade Organisation in that city, through the globally coordinated mass protests of the anti-war movement at the turn of the century opposing American empire, through to political insurgencies within domestic party systems in the form of left populism by the second decade of the century, taking place either within old social democratic parties (in the UK and US) or against them (Spain, Greece, France), the left has fled the ether of transnational civil society back to the confines of national politics.

From having renounced the parochialism and rigidity of mere party politics on the eve of the millennium, by the end of the twenty-year crisis the left was confronting the outer limits to their electoral insurgencies, as indicated in the poor showing of left populist parties in the continental elections to the European Parliament in May 2019. The full story of this political evolution – or indeed the dialectic between national and international politics – is beyond the scope of this book. What is important for our purposes here is how this shift from global supranationalism through to national populism intersected with critical and radical international theories, as we shall see in more detail in the next chapter. Suffice to say here that the failures of the left are constitutive of the twenty-year crisis inasmuch as their failure to surmount the crisis inevitably means that they have been at its mercy. The global trade talks to which the protestors at Seattle were so vehemently opposed in 1999 failed not because of the strength of the opposition to them, but of their own accord, foundering on the question of agricultural subsidies in the advanced economies. The so-called Uruguay round of multilateral trade negotiations that were completed in 1995 was the final successful round of such negotiations; the Doha round of talks that began in 2001 have never been consummated. Arguably, we all live in the backwash of these failed trade talks, as the high tide of global capitalism has receded, forcing everyone to retreat into a more fragmented and fractious global economy. As we shall see in greater detail, the left, and Critical IR more generally, never managed successfully to navigate the ebb and flow of the tides of unipolar globalisation.

Of all these developments, however, the two most important events that we can say precipitated the start of our twenty-years' crisis were, first, the formal founding of the EU currency, the euro, that year, which was introduced to global currency markets on 1 January 1999, when it replaced the "ecu" as the currency of eleven EU member states; 2019 was the tenth anniversary of the Eurozone crisis that erupted in Greece in late 2009. The second event was the Kosovo War in which NATO, while expanding eastwards, also launched a war on its southern flank against the rump-Yugoslav state, to halt the counter-insurgency campaign being waged against Kosovar Albanian separatists by the federal government in Belgrade. Much like the Versailles peace settlement of 1919 laid the foundations for the crisis of the 1930s, so too 1999 laid the foundations of our contemporary crisis: the hardening of Eutopianism as it was carried through from politics to economics in the establishment of a monetary union without a fiscal union, and with the Kosovo War, the start of inverted revisionism, in which the leading liberal powers mined the foundations of their own international order. The collapse in early 2019 of the war crimes trial of ex-Ivorian leader Laurent Gbagbo at the International Criminal Court (ICC) in The Hague underscores the end of this cycle of cosmopolitan liberalism, the Court itself having been established just before the start of our twenty years' crisis with the Rome Statute of 1998. With the failure of the ICC twenty years on, we might do well to recall the Hegelian dictum endorsed by Carr that "world history is the world court."[39] Our twenty years' crisis thus begins in 1999. Eutopianism will be considered in more detail in chapter 3. Here we will consider the implication of the Kosovo War for international order and security.

Inverted Revisionism and Humanitarian War

Although the old Socialist Federal Republic of Yugoslavia had not been part of the Soviet empire in Eastern Europe, paradoxically the disintegration of the Yugoslav federation paralleled that of the USSR at the end of the Cold War. Thus NATO intervention in the name of human rights in the internal affairs of a national government seeking to crush ethnic separatists in Kosovo would inevitably stir anxiety in Moscow as well as in Beijing and Delhi, all fearful of their own restive peripheral minorities. Indeed, the abiding Indian suspicion of humanitarian intervention always complicated the attempt to depict human rights as the cause of global democracy. That the world's largest democracy persistently indicated its suspicion of and hostility towards the new Western militarism vindicates Carr inasmuch as it illustrates the power politics that undergird soaring normative aspirations. Important as this was, however, the significance of the Kosovo War went beyond stoking great-power tensions in Europe or on the UN Security Council.

Unlike previous crises of post-Cold War intervention, the Kosovo War proceeded both without any invitation or assent of the Yugoslav state and without UN authorisation, and thus without Sino-Russian assent (NATO forces would go on to bomb the Chinese embassy in Belgrade for good measure). While humanitarian justifications for military intervention had already become the weapon of choice in the West's ideological arsenal when fighting its new imperial bush wars in Somalia (1992), Bosnia-Herzegovina (1995) and Sierra Leone (1998), the fact that Yugoslav sovereignty was violated and international law subverted was highly significant, for this embodied a new paradigm of "sovereignty as responsibility" to substitute for the idea of sovereignty as autonomy. British Prime Minister Tony Blair cast the conflict in the grandest and most idealistic terms imaginable – as an epochal struggle "between good and evil, between civilisation and barbarity; between democracy and dictatorship."[40] Here NATO was conjuring a form of political and legal authority that went higher than any actually existing political or legal institution, that justified aggressive war and that necessarily relegated the rights of states in favour of a nebulous conception of humanity that could be easily moulded around the needs of Western power.

There was much here that a Carrian could have razored apart. As Brian Porter has noted, in many ways Western intervention since the end of the Cold War could be seen as "Daviesian" – that is, as following the prescriptions of Welsh politician Lord David Davies, Carr's nemesis during the time that Carr held the Woodrow Wilson Chair at Aberystwyth during the interbellum. A committed liberal utopian of the interwar variety, Davies's hope for a powerfully armed, speedy international police force of the air, as outlined in his 1930 book *The Problem of the Twentieth Century*, was seemingly vindicated in the era of humanitarian intervention. Despite the fact that Carr was read on every IR undergraduate syllabus and Davies was not, the posthumous political triumph of Davies over Carr would suggest that Carr's insights had been lost somewhere en route.[41] Indeed, many of those scholars explicitly claiming Carr's legacy supported humanitarian intervention and actively theorised it.[42] It was left to political realists such as the butcher of Cambodia himself, Dr Henry Kissinger, to make arguments against the Kosovo intervention that were more critical than the supposed critical theorists' were – although Kissinger was much more invested in maintaining the West's international position than Carr would have been. Thus, for all the critical theorists' claim to be critical, few were willing to deploy "theories as weapons," as Carr would have had it, to actually criticise the powerful states, as Carr was happy to do. Thus constructivists, solidarists, critical theorists, post-structuralists all aligned behind the liberal crusade, a powerful indication of the new strain of utopianism in IR in which power, self-interest and norms all became intermingled and normative ideals were no longer seen as power political.

The ramifications of the Kosovo War were extensive: the war precipitated the establishment of a new model of "sovereignty as responsibility," in which grandiose hopes for enshrining human rights at the global level predictably collapsed into a new legitimation of state power with no corresponding improvement in human rights guarantees.[43] It provided the military template for the "new liberal way of war" that would be applied later in the Greater Middle East: an air campaign by Western states supported on the ground by proxy ethnic militias bolstered by cosmopolitan jihadi shock troops. The international protectorate established over Kosovo following the end of the war perpetuated a new model of trusteeship in which international institutions annexed the governance of various territories and populations. In some respects, this new trusteeship was even worse than the mandates system of the interbellum – not least because the new trusteeship was said to be legally and politically compatible with self-determination.[44]

Kosovo also helped legitimate Russian revanchism and military intervention. The NATO-sponsored ethnic cleansing of Kosovo through which it was emptied of most of its Serbian and Roma minority in repeat pogroms after the war, and its subsequent declaration of independence in 2008, established the precedent of revising borders in Europe. Thus, after Kosovo declared independence in 2008, the pro-Russian enclaves of Abkhazia and South Ossetia would declare their independence from Georgia while citing the Kosovo precedent, as indeed would Crimea when its local authorities seceded from Ukraine in 2014 before being absorbed by Russia. Perhaps most important of all, Kosovo set the stage for Iraq: most of those who loudly inveighed against intervention in Iraq had supported the intervention over Kosovo. Intervention followed the same pattern, claiming rights of intervention over the rights of state sovereignty, strongly justified in humanitarian terms of ending tyranny, and doing so without the political support of the UN Security Council. While many humanitarian theorists have sought to firewall Iraq from interventions they supported, there was no escaping the clear political conclusion: Kosovo made the full-scale invasion of Iraq possible.[45] All of this would be consistent with a Carrian analysis.

In some respects, this new liberal humanitarian utopianism went beyond Carr's analysis however. While a Carrian would be led to suspect that all grand declarations of universal interest and benevolence are but "unconscious reflexions" of national self-interest at any particular time, they would be hard-pressed to find any solid core of hard strategic necessity or political self-interest in the intervention in Kosovo. If the historic claim of liberal internationalism was a rules-based order founded on the universal good around which collective management of common interests could be organised, then Kosovo represented something novel. Here, established, status quo powers were not only openly flouting the UN Charter with respect to non-interference in the internal affairs of member states, but also flouting the will of the UN Security Council.

In other words, they were not only undermining the concrete expression of their rules and institutions, but in claiming higher rights to do so, they were undercutting the very notion of an international order organised around a stable set of expectations, norms and laws. It was emerging powers – China, India, Russia – on the other hand, those who could be closer to Carr's have-nots in our own day, who were thrust into the position of being conservative defenders of the status quo. Indeed, China and Russia in particular were cast in the role of deviants for being *insufficiently* revisionist – they were the so-called Westphalian powers, clinging to outmoded ideals of sovereignty stemming from an obsolete, Eurocentric seventeenth-century system of peace treaties. Thus we had have-not powers defending states' rights to non-intervention in the face of the grand claims made for human rights by the status quo powers. It was, in short, a mirror-image of Carr's depiction of the interbellum. Kosovo thus established a new pattern of international politics – leading status quo powers invoking a new armed doctrine of liberal utopianism to undermine *their own* order, thereby establishing one of the crucial dynamics of the Twenty Years' Crisis of the twenty-first century. In place of pursuing a magnanimous victory and simply maintaining a largely pacified international order once the proxy wars of the Cold War era had burned themselves out, liberal states instead explicitly chose a strategy of using force and power to reshape that very same order: sanctions, humanitarian intervention, democracy promotion, state-building, air strikes and targeted assassinations all became par for the course.

The Critique of the Twenty Years' Crisis, 1939–2019

The differences between the interbellum and our own era are many, and adumbrating them here should help to clarify what is specific about the liberal international order now receding into the past and why it is in crisis. Carr was very clear that global leadership was in abeyance in his era, as British supremacy in the nineteenth century was eroded. To Carr's mind, the liberal idea of "collective interest" in the interbellum testified to an unstable multipolar order, in which vague universality was invoked to substitute for the supposedly spontaneous "harmony of interests" of the prior generation – the earlier harmony that had in fact been nothing more than the operation of the gold standard backed up by British sea-power. As we have seen, in Carr's view the injustice and naivety of the Paris peace settlement and its associated system of global treaties created a hierarchy bifurcated between the "haves" – the British, French and US – and the "have-nots," excluded, subjugated or dissatisfied to varying degrees and in different ways – the Italians, Japanese and especially Germans. These were the powers excluded from the spoils of the victors' peace, who were thus inevitably cast in the role of insurgents against the status quo, as they were the ones with the most direct interest and incentive to reshape the existing international order – thus the Italians bombed Corfu in 1923, the Japanese encroached on Manchuria across the 1930s, while "Germany reconstituted *Mittel-Europa* and pressed forward into the Balkans."[46]

What made the Wilsonian peace settlement that much more rigid and consequently brittle was the fact that it was buttressed with morally charged liberal utopian hopes. Despite being an order resting ultimately on Anglo-French military power and US wealth through a feedback loop of US dollar loans to Europe, force was abjured and a tremendous degree of authority was vested in the power of public opinion, as well as in the respect accorded to sovereign self-determination.[47] This emphasis on self-determination irked Carr greatly, as he saw in state sovereignty "a principle of political disintegration"[48] that tugged against the powerful undertow of "technical, industrial and economic development" – forces that Carr saw as dictating "a progressive increase in the size of the effective political unit."[49] He found the "old national unit ... intolerably restrictive" and especially so in Europe, precisely because of Europe's lead in fields such as infrastructure and

communications.[50] Thus Carr heaped contempt on the political aspirations of the new nations of Central and Eastern Europe, which he
regarded as fragile monuments to Wilsonian folly – despite the fact
that the system of minority treaties piled upon the newly independent
states of the region as well as the neocolonial mandates system outside
of Europe all gave the lie to the idea that these new states enjoyed the
same sovereign rights as the old states of Europe.

All of this was then packaged in a new conception of international
law, which Carr castigated as exhibiting a fetishistic style of thinking
that failed to grasp the fluidity of politics and the reality of state power,
especially as German strength grew inexorably from its nadir in 1919.
Against the naive hopes placed in the reverence for international justice, law and the power of public opinion, Carr argued cogently and
forcefully that, even from the viewpoint of maintaining peace, force
could not be abjured because the deterrent effect of threats of force
were necessary, precisely to effect peaceful change. Without it, the ex-
hortations to peace were merely empty.

The dynamics that were eroding this liberal order Carr saw as large
mega-trends, such as demographic growth, industrialisation and the
massification of politics, as the extension of the franchise led to the
absorption of the urban and industrial working classes into national
politics.[51] Although Carr approvingly intoned Lenin, he took the Tory
prime minister Benjamin Disraeli and the firmly anti-Marxist Prussian
chancellor Otto von Bismarck as the great nation-building statesmen
whose national policies and extensions of the franchise in the nineteenth century laid the grounds for twentieth-century politics.

What then are the forces eroding our own liberal order? As we have
already seen, the insurgents against this order have been the leading
liberal states rather than our emerging powers. Carr noted that "the
growing strength of the United States in international trade and finance was one, at any rate, of the reasons which allowed the United
States Government to abandon its traditional practice of landing
marines in the recalcitrant Latin American republics and to adopt the
'good neighbour' policy."[52] By this standard then, the number and intensity of military interventions in recent times would lead us to believe that US power is precipitously declining. Yet the US economy
remains at the core of the global order. Russian revanchism of recent
times might be more explicable in terms of weakness, too, rather than
surging strength. That is, despite its strategic success, we could quite

plausibly see Russia's use of force more as an expression of weakness than strength, a reactive lashing back at the successive waves of NATO and EU expansion now lapping at its borders. Arguably Russia's partial strategic successes in Syria and Ukraine reflect weakness that forces the Russian government into clear-sighted decisions and trade-offs in a way that the liberal "have" powers seem to be incapable of. Moreover, it is worth remembering that, unlike inter-war Germany, Russia's renewed assertiveness is a function of fluctuations in the price of oil rather than a reflection of growing industrial strength, demographic growth, enhanced economic productivity or technological advances.

From this perspective, Western intervention remains peculiar, and while Kosovo represents a turning point for reasons already discussed above, the new interventionism did indeed begin with the return of US marines to Latin America – that is, with the 1989 intervention in Panama. That the "haves," the status quo powers, are now corroding their own order from within suggests an entirely new category of revisionist behaviour – what I have labelled elsewhere "inverted revisionism."[53] While Carr would fully expect great powers to flout international law, he would not have expected satisfied powers to do so.[54] Today, we have seen cardinal principles of international law such as non-intervention, non-aggression and the supremacy of the UN Security Council systematically corroded. This certainly seems at odds with the pathetic clinging to the Franco-American Kellog-Briand Pact of 1928 that risibly sought to ban war, or the populist veneration of the League that was witnessed in the interbellum. Moreover, inverted revisionism was all undertaken in the name of a higher law – a cosmopolitan political vision of supranational politics and transnational law to supplant institutions based on inter-state mediation and political pluralism. In this new order, the interests of cosmopolitan humanity would substitute for state interests. This was a new "harmony of interests" raised above a mere coalescence of state interests, and was at once more ethereal and militaristic than anything seen in Carr's day.

Similarly, whereas Carr castigated the liberals of the interbellum for their supposed attachment to sovereignty, it would be hard to charge post-Cold War liberals with the same sin – quite the opposite. The disparagement of sovereign statehood has been the most abiding characteristic of our liberal utopians across our twenty years' crisis, and indeed the whole post-Cold War period. Sovereign rights have been repudiated in the name of human rights, democratisation, regional and even global integration. As we have seen, liberals of our era have been as derisory towards the sovereignty of small Balkan nations as Carr, who haughtily derided the internecine "conflicts and jealousies" of "Danubian politics after 1919."[55] Today Carr's disdain for sovereignty would find him in the camp of liberals, not outside it.

The other striking element of the contemporary liberal international order that clashes with that of the interbellum is the attitude to public opinion. Carr scorned this as a platitudinous reverence. Keenly aware of the fact that political power was more than crude measures of national strength such as coal or steel output and that it was dependent on belief and legitimacy, he nonetheless despised the liberal invocation of public opinion, feeling that in an age of mass politics and systematically produced and disseminated propaganda, the notion of an autonomously formed public opinion independent of state power was meaningless. On the international stage, invoking the power of public opinion became the quintessential "unconscious reflexion" of national interest, and the slogans of "League enthusiasts" such as "peace and disarmament" could only exist, according to Carr, because they meant "different and indeed contrasting things to different people."[56]

Today, by contrast, liberal leaders stand out by defining themselves by their resistance to popular pressure and public opinion. Perhaps the most iconic example of this was British prime minister Tony Blair who wore his unpopularity over the Iraq war as a badge of honour, proof that his premiership was not defined by opinion polls but by conviction – conviction that ironically could only be given meaning by being defined against the populace.[57] Neo-conservatives and theorists of humanitarian intervention have persistently taken the lack of broad and deep public support for their military adventures as indicative of democratic materialism – that is, as evidence of an apathetic populace, too addled by consumerism and narrow self-interest to take up the task of global crusading on behalf of democracy and human rights.[58] Thus the cosmopolitan vision of human rights served the dual purpose of deriding democracy at home while subjugating Third World nations abroad.

Elsewhere, liberal internationalists and NATO enthusiasts have consistently expressed their frustration over the stubbornness of the German public in refusing to express sufficient belligerence towards Russia – something that any rational observer, in light of the twentieth century, might be willing to consider as a positive.[59] The anti-plebeian fury of Britain's Brahmin classes in response to the majority decision in the Brexit referendum of 2016 was also evidence of how detached liberal politics has become. Thus what is striking about contemporary liberalism is that it is so defined against public opinion, as is evident in the sagging opinion polls of deeply unpopular leaders such as French president Emmanuel Macron, who has defined himself as restoring the liberal centre. Too late, the liberal *Economist* understood that liberal unpopularity had been the decisive characteristic of the twenty years' crisis, thereby hollowing out popular support for liberalism in both domestic and international politics:

> All too often, in recent years, liberal reforms have been imposed by judges, by central banks and by unaccountable supranational organisations. Perhaps the best-founded part of today's reaction against liberalism is the outrage people feel when its nostrums are imposed on them with condescending promises that they will be the better for it.[60]

If one of Carr's conclusions was that liberalism was ill-suited to an age of mass politics, perhaps our conclusion would be that liberalism is also clearly unsustainable *without* mass politics.

The contrast is instructive. Liberal internationalism is once again fomenting disorder, albeit in very different ways. For Carr, liberal idealism rigidified the international order, making peaceful change more difficult by limiting political flexibility and fostering idealistic delusions. If these charges could be collectively levelled at the liberal international order once again, the targets would be different: political flexibility has indeed been limited by idealistic delusions such as the Eurozone, but peaceful change has been substituted by a profound ideological commitment to perpetual war. Revisionism is now the prototypical behaviour of the liberal powers rather than the have-nots; and the idealism is that of supranational human rights that justifies trampling the self-determination of small nations. Far from enforcing or revering rules, it has been liberals who have abjured them, all in the name of a higher order of which they are at once both the prophets and avenging angels. In all its various incarnations, such as human rights, humanitarianism, peacekeeping, democratisation and state-building, liberal internationalism has become militarised and globalised, scaled up into cosmopolitanism. There is perhaps an inkling of this liberal revisionism in Carr's

Twenty Years' Crisis, which would indeed be consistent with Carr's own position as a member (albeit a maverick member) of the British foreign policy elite. As a Cambridge classicist, seasoned diplomat and participant in the Paris peace conferences as well as a regular leader writer for *The Times*, perhaps it was the ultimate challenge of accommodating US power that exercised Carr more than the revisionist policies of Germany. After all, the globalised ultra-revisionism of the US, draped in the mantle of liberal idealism, posed a direct challenge to Britain's leading global role in a way that far surpassed the more modest challenge of German power.[61] The task for the analyst then as now was to unmask the power political content of liberalism.

Nonetheless, while Carr exaggerated the pacifism of the Wilsonian vision of collective security, there was little doubt that the League's formal commitment to peaceful international order was greater than that of the post-war and especially the post-Cold War UN order. The UN has had much more persistent recourse to force and coercion, not only in the record of sanctions that have been far more damaging, not to say murderous, when compared to the ineffectual sanctions of Carr's day, but also in the militarisation of UN peacekeeping, which has seen large military deployments become coterminous with peace agreements, leading to global military deployments on a scale exceeded only by that of the US itself.[62] It is difficult to imagine a more thoroughgoing inversion of the IR categories of the interbellum, which would have us associate liberalism with naive hopes for peace and realism with a ruthless penchant for war. Instead, today liberal internationalism has become the doctrine of permanent war.

Conclusion

As we have seen, undertaking historical comparisons is a complex task, there being at least as many significant points of difference as resemblances. The contrast is nonetheless informative, because it makes us consider how both international order and liberal internationalism have developed over the last century. The crises that we confront seem to be the same as those confronting Carr – intertwined crises of democracy, self-determination and market economics. Yet in some respects the irrationality of contemporary politics seems at once deeper and stranger. Whereas Carr charged the liberals of his own day with inuring themselves to the reality of political change in their determination to preserve the flawed Versailles settlement, the liberals of our own twenty years' crisis have squandered the geopolitical gains of their victory in the Cold War through a programme of attempted systemic transformation. Our liberal utopians have made conflict a permanent feature of the contemporary order, undermining the very rules they established to govern themselves and the rest of the world. Liberalism was supposed to stand for self-determination, anti-imperialism, collective coordination through international organisation, the sanctity of international law, peace through international trade, cooperation and civil society. The liberalism of our era has undermined all of these, scorning self-determination in favour of supranationalism and neo-trusteeship, while seeing peace as a product of the effective deployment of military power in the form of blue helmets. All of this smacks of regression in liberalism, for at least the liberal idealists of Carr's day could claim a redeeming nobility of purpose. Surveying the menagerie of new protectorates and various theatres of the forever war stretching across the Balkans and Middle East, respectively, it would be difficult to identify any redeeming value in early-twenty-first-century liberal utopianism.

Carr looked forward to the end of liberalism and coolly claimed that one prediction could "be made with confidence," namely that the "concept of sovereignty is likely to became in the future even more blurred and indistinct than it is at present."[63] In Carr's view, the rickety superstructure of Woodrow Wilson's Ruritanian international order of fragmented sovereign states was crumbling away as the tectonic plates of international power shifted, revealing vast autarkic new power blocs centred around the US, USSR, Germany, Britain and Japan. Extrapolating from this, Carr reasoned that if the British bourgeoisie could come to take the "welfare of Oldham or Jarrow" into account, "the less difficult," he suggested, "will it seem to realise that these social ends cannot be limited by a national frontier." If the British capitalists could see that their interests were served by uplifting Britain's industrial working class, why could this sentiment not extend beyond borders? For if labour and capital could be reconciled within states, why could tensions between states also not be superseded? Fused together, the working class and capitalist class could "broaden our view of international policy" to "take into account the welfare of Lille or Düsseldorf or Lodz as well as the welfare of Oldham or Jarrow."[64] Thus Carr believed that the collective solidarities of mass national politics would submerge not only the liberal individualism and class-based socialism of the nineteenth century, but were also now sufficiently powerful and cohesive to burst apart the nation-state and thrust upwards towards a supranational political system overseen by continental agencies of economic planning and regulation.

Since the end of the Cold War and long after the interbellum, Łódź and Düsseldorf have adapted to the post-industrial economy of Europe, Jarrow and Oldham perhaps less so. Today, instead of autarkic power blocs carving up the liberal international order between them, we have a densely intermeshed global economy with trade at the pre-interbellum heights of the *Belle Époque* now being rent by the centrifugal forces of sovereign states. The US is restlessly churning within its regional and global trading blocs of NAFTA and the WTO; Hungary seeks to pull central and Eastern European member states into a new illiberal alliance within the EU; Italy is weighed down by its debts while straining against the Eurozone;, and of course Britain struggles to extricate itself from the EU. Far from the industrial working classes having been successfully integrated into national life, the rump industrial working class – those whom Hillary Clinton called the "deplorables" – have been repelled from political life in the US, Britain, France, Italy, while the so-called new working class is no less alienated.[65] Indeed, I would go further and say that this demassification of politics is a precondition of transnational integration today, as we shall see in more detail in chapter 3. Thus, instead of nineteenth-century liberalism being swallowed up by collective solidarity at the national level as Carr expected, what we have instead is liberalism evaporating into the void where collective solidarities used to be. Against Carr's expectations, transnational solidarity has come at the expense of, and not been built on, national cohesion and solidarity.

Today, political realism would perforce draw our attention to the reality of fragmented political systems internal to nation states, at least in the most advanced capitalist countries of the West. The political realism of our time is not the solidarity of the nation state exploding liberal international order, but its internal weaknesses no longer providing a solid foundation for liberal international order, let alone the grand pan-European, transnational integration envisaged by Carr. In our own time, national sovereignty remains the only viable political container for the collective solidarity that Carr expected would burst apart the sovereign nation-state. If our future is a multipolar one it is not one of competing regional power blocs but competing powerful states – China, the US, Japan, India, Russia, Brazil ... Only Europe would need to become a transnational regional power bloc to compete in this world, but then again only a Eutopian would see the necessity of propelling Europe towards such a confrontation.

One aspect of liberal international order that we have not addressed explicitly is the fact that interbellum comparisons are *also* a component of liberal international order. Indeed, how could it be otherwise, given that the UN order was built on the ruins of the League? Perhaps the surest sign of the resilience of the liberal international order is the recurrent ritual of invoking the interbellum as the past to be warded off by incanting the failures of the League, the failures of appeasement, the failures to coordinate policy in the Great Depression, and so on. The interbellum thus functions as the vindication of the contemporary order. On the one hand, the interbellum is presented as the primitive first installment from which we learned and subsequently collectively upgraded our institutions, while at the same time elements of the interbellum seem to act like a lingering malicious code or glitch that threaten to bring the system crashing down. Nearly a century later, how might we wipe the interbellum from the system?

2 Make IR Critical Again

No one wants to be a liberal. IR – especially British IR – includes constructivists, critical realists (not to be confused with the plain old realists), historical sociologists, queer theorists, solidarists, critical constructivists, poststructuralists, Marxists, feminists, decolonialists, cosmopolitans, post-colonialists, Bourdieusians, critical race theorists, political economists, post-humanists, practice theorists, Gramscians, the new old-fashioned classical realists, Foucauldians, and any number of critical, neo-, post- and hybrid varieties of these strains. Given all this lush profusion, who would wish to stand for such mundane notions as individual rights, freedom, autonomy, universalism and markets? Indeed, not even liberals themselves, as today they tend to prefer human rights to citizens' rights, peacekeepers to soldiers, interdependence to independence, judges to elected representatives, trusteeship to self-determination, supranational authority to the liberal nation-state ... Stephen M. Walt and John J. Mearsheimer have forcefully criticised policies of liberal hegemony for ushering in the age of permanent war after the end of the Cold War. Criticising liberal hegemonies of various kinds and along various lines has also long been the staple of Critical IR. So what would Carr's critique of inter-war liberalism offer to us today, given the plethora of already existing criticisms of liberalism?

Despite the theoretical variety and putative opposition to liberal hegemony (as well as neoliberalism), it is noteworthy that all these vigorous critical theoretical strains seem to leave little trace in international politics. That is, they fail to exhibit any concrete *political* alternatives, but merely flaunt their intellectual variety. In short, there is a tremendous discrepancy between IR's theoretical fecundity and its actual political uniformity. This has been particularly exposed over the last few years. As the foundations of the liberal international order began to shake, everyone scurried to the shelter of the temple. As a discipline, IR preferred Hillary Clinton to Donald Trump, the EU to Brexit, cosmopolitan jihadism to Bashar al-Assad, the Eurozone to Grexit, NATO to Vladimir Putin, Emmanuel Macron to the *gilets jaunes*. The purpose of this chapter is to explain how the new liberal utopianism manifests itself in unexpected places. As we shall see, on closer inspection, the battered, grand old temple of liberal international order is held aloft by critical-IR perspectives, which are thickly entwined around its crumbling pillars and growing in its many moist cracks and crevices.

New Liberal Utopianisms

I argued in previous chapters that utopianism had to be understood differently than in Carr's day, not least because of the fact that, theoretically speaking, liberal influence over the academy is not as great as it was in Carr's day. However, one of the contentions of this book is that IR theories have been through so many intellectual turns now – the "linguistic turn," the "Gramscian turn," the "Foucauldian turn," the "cultural turn," the "visual turn," the "practice turn," the "local turn," the "spatial turn," the "everyday turn" – that we have turned ourselves back to where we started, squarely located in liberal utopianism, as well as now being dizzy from all that spinning.[1] Although IR is a more complex field than in the past, with more contention between various theoretical approaches, given that its politics is still essentially that of liberal utopianism how did this strain grow back from seemingly different theoretical roots? In this chapter, I propose to examine two of those roots, albeit particularly thick and deep ones – critical theory and constructivism. Although the two theories are frequently seen as distinctive, with constructivism being more established and orthodox whereas critical theory, allegedly, remains more heterodox, I want to show that both theoretical strands are utopian in the sense that Carr meant – despite the fact that both have defined themselves against liberal internationalism. Nonetheless, I argue, they are utopian in the basic sense that they are "unconscious reflexions" of power and interest, despite – or perhaps even because – they explicitly cast themselves as critical of existing power structures. They are also utopian in that they neglect the factor of (state) power and overestimate the possibilities for voluntarily reshaping international politics. As a result, they end up essentially affirming contemporary international order: both constructivist and critical theoretical approaches have blossomed in the soil of US unipolar power, and, as we shall see, it is an environment that they find exceptionally hospitable.

Needless to say, I am far from being the first to criticise these theoretical approaches for their complicity with existing power structures.[2] Nor am I the first to claim that constructivism and critical theory are latter-day strains of liberal idealism.[3] I wish to go further here, however, and suggest that critical theories quite clearly expresses the utopianism analysed by Carr. Indeed, I would hazard to say that the intellectual and institutional resilience of critical theories in IR – despite having been subject to excoriating critiques across the 1990s – shows the complementarity of these theories with liberal international order; they serve a purpose.[4] However, not only is this political accommodation guiltily disguised by radical theorising, it also represents an historic intellectual failure – with grave consequences, the failure in which they fell short of the very standards that they set themselves.

The great claim of constructivist and critical theory was offering a way to conceptualise purposive change – to "denaturalise" the international order, to show that it was not governed by insuperable natural laws but by human artifice. Thus, both constructivist and critical theory explicitly cast themselves in a libratory mould, teaching us that the status quo need not be accepted as the "natural order" of things. But what happens when they become simply utopians of the status quo?

Both critical theorists and constructivists were focussed on change, not stasis, and with the change came the possibility of improvement. As theoretical frameworks, they both cast themselves against the rigidity of structural and rationalist approaches, mostly closely associated with neo-realism and, to a lesser extent, neoliberalism. Both critical theoretical and constructivist approaches profited intellectually from the end of the Cold War, when what had hitherto appeared as a rigid structure – the Cold War bipolar system – simply melted away. Both theoretical frameworks were defined against sanctifying the status quo. Both – especially constructivists – sought to vault off the end of the Cold War to explain how they might construct a positive feedback loop in which their theoretically reasoned, empirically tested insights into change would, in turn, improve the direction and tempo of change. In effect, constructivism promised nothing less than a virtuous upward spiral, in which constructivist theory would boost international politics onto a qualitatively improved level, which would in turn spiral upwards through yet more constructivist theory ... International order, a human artefact after all, would not be taken as a given, natural order, but one susceptible to willed change. This is the implication of the idea that society and by extension international order is a "social construct" – something confected, artificial, and assembled from pre-existing elements. Steeped in the outlook of transformation, agency and predicated on the fundamental malleability of social life, how did these theories come to be so affirmative of the extant order? What is at stake then is not merely the relative standing of various theories, nor even the political standing of states, but rather how we understand the possibility of changing world order. The failure of constructivism and critical theory to consummate this project of progressive change means that the task of "denaturalisation" still awaits us.

Post-Cold War international relations theory comprises many roots and branches, but in this chapter my focus is only on critical theory and constructivism because I think they constitute some of the thickest and strongest roots of the whole structure of the new utopianism today. Hacking at the root inevitably means tearing through plenty of lush foliage above. What is offered below is thus neither a comprehensive account nor a critique of either constructivism or critical theory in IR. Rather, my purpose is to show how both theories, in seeking to conceptualise change, undercut their own premises and collapse into a new utopianism of the status quo, thereby undermining the possibility for progressive political change. I also restrict my focus to a few iconic and hugely influential texts and thinkers – such as those of Alexander Wendt and Emmanuel Adler, but especially the late Robert Cox. This is because I feel that a close and careful engagement with paradigmatic texts serves our purposes better in identifying the taproots of latter-day liberal utopianism than attempting a comprehensive taxonomy of a vast and complex field before mounting a critique. While there is already critical engagement with critical scholarship, I also believe that earlier critiques of these "critical critics" has not penetrated sufficiently deeply. Beate Jahn, for instance, in her otherwise ruthless assessment of Critical IR from 1998, spares Robert Cox.[5] Here, by contrast, I want to show that the utopian roots do indeed run down that far, if not further.

If we consider constructivism, then we have to acknowledge Alexander Wendt as among the most prolific, stimulating and innovative IR theorists of the twenty years' crisis; indeed, his classic text, *Social Theory of International Politics*, was published at the start of the crisis, in 1999. Since then, he has discussed both the implications of the findings of quantum physics for social science as well as seeking to restore teleology to political theory and boldly predicting a future world-state.[6] In this chapter, we shall be considering his earlier analyses of change in the international system, as well as some constructivist fellow travellers. Cox, on the other hand is, like Carr, one of those thinkers condemned to be cited more than read, especially by way of absolutising the former's distinction between problem-solving and critical theory, thereby missing the context and qualifications with which Cox hedged this (admittedly problematic) distinction. The Internet has absorbed countless studies proclaiming their intellectual superiority to all existing scholarship through invoking Cox's distinction. Also not unlike Carr, Cox's work from the twentieth century has many uncanny echoes and harbingers of the present. Cox's remarkable account of the transnationalisation of the state as horizontal, lateral linkages binding together fragments of the old nation-state in new cross-border configurations will be considered in the next chapter on Eutopianism. Here we will only consider Cox's broad accounts of theorising international order.

Constructing the New Utopianism

As the name suggests, the basic and most powerful insight and claim of constructivist thought, broadly conceived, is the notion that the social world is a human product and that, as a result, nothing can be taken for granted or need be simply accepted as "the way things are."[7] To extend and scale up these insights from the malleability of domestic social order to the international plane was a bold intellectual leap.[8] To be sure, the "naturalness" of the international order had already been scrambled by the mid-twentieth century. This happened first with the collapse in the interbellum of the great nineteenth-century liberal global economy, whose disintegration underscored that the market could not be seen as having the spontaneity of a natural order. The second moment came when the Japanese nearly destroyed the US Pacific Fleet at Pearl Harbour in December 1941 and seized the supposedly impregnable naval fortress of Singapore from the British in early 1942. These military victories signalled the annihilation of white supremacy, and with it the defeat of the notion that biological hierarchy could be inscribed into international order.[9]

However, the Cold War-era world of nuclear and geopolitical rivalries, of superpower stalemate, of inexorably escalating arms races and seemingly monolithic alliance systems still appeared to be plagued by dynamics that, even if social rather than biological, as racial hierarchy was supposed to be, nonetheless appeared structurally embedded and insurmountable. Yet this did not halt the application of constructivist ideas to the international realm, with Alexander Wendt boldly proclaiming that "anarchy is what states make of it" as early as 1992.[10] To contest what appeared to be the defining, structuring principle of international politics – the absence of a central government to impose order – and to claim that it need not be taken as an ineluctable fact analogous to a law of nature, was a bold move indeed.

Constructivists mobilised a formidable range of sophisticated ideas to mount their challenge to the status quo powers of IR theory. Their "theoretical weapons," to borrow Carr's phrase, ranged from Weberian sociology through symbolic interactionism to social psychology and the philosophy of language, among other approaches. Early constructivist efforts could be traced back to Karl Deutsch's work of the early Cold War era on the idea of forging "security communities" in the West. In these security communities, common problems could be jointly managed through institutionalised reciprocity that would help consolidate trust, mutual understanding and sympathy, that would in turn be the basis of community between nations.[11] Yet as long as the bipolar system of the Cold War persisted, the notion of a "security community" could only ever be an ideological gloss on "the West," an intellectual shield for NATO in its stand-off with the Warsaw Pact. Thus, despite occasional constructivist stirring during the glacial era of the second Cold War during the 1980s, it was only with the end of the Cold War as a whole and the liquidation of bipolar geopolitics that constructivism could flourish and even come to supplant, if not entirely displace, the earlier orthodoxy in the Anglo-American academy, structural realism.

Although structural realism could conceive of change within states and variation in foreign policy, it held that the structure of power political competition in international order would curb states to a limited range of behaviour that would recur and repeat over time.[12] The failure to predict the end of the Cold War was thus a serious blow to the predictive claims and hence the scientific credibility of structural realism. While structural realists could credibly claim that they could only predict broad recurring patterns of international politics rather than singularities like the end of the Cold War, this intellectual rearguard manoeuvre was insufficient. Not only did a host of ancillary realist predictions – nuclear proliferation in Europe, the disintegration of NATO, France pursuing new balance of power strategies in Eastern Europe – fail to materialise, but constructivists could also credibly claim to have not only substantive but positively progressive accounts of the changes being witnessed. Transforming supposedly interdependent structures of political identity and complexes of ideas could, they claimed, help to explain events such as the end of apartheid in South Africa or the development of Mikhail Gorbachev's "New Thinking in Foreign Policy" which would help to melt the Cold War frost. The rapidity of international change without, say, a drastic cut in one side's number of tanks or nuclear missiles, the absence of world war, the apparent centrality of liberal ideas and human rights to these changes; the fall of fearsome, enclosed dictatorships to international pressure and popular mobilisation – all these developments militated for constructivist ideas. Broadly understood, the reciprocal interaction of bottom-up agency – street protests, civic struggles – and top-down transformations of international-level social structure (such as Gorbachev's "New Thinking") could produce self-reinforcing virtuous cycles of social change and progressive improvement.[13]

In the so-called paradigm wars of the 1980s and '90s, the constructivists were cast as one of the multiple theoretical insurgencies warring amongst themselves while also challenging the orthodoxy of structural realism, which supposedly buttressed the status quo. Yet constructivists' views of international change complemented US and Western foreign policy in the aftermath of the Cold War, broadly supporting liberalisation, democratisation, the diffusion of human rights and the deepening of global civil society. All of these were part of transforming not only states but also the international order itself. While structural realists compared international order to the market that standardises behaviour among profit-maximising firms through the discipline of competition, constructivists invoked the entrepreneur, who could not only remake firms but remake the market itself. In the international political context, these were the so-called norm entrepreneurs – typically NGOs, but also, variously, the social democratic Scandinavian states and the European Union – actors who would, in this neo-liberalised variant of IR theory remade for globalising capitalism, nimbly innovate their way around the lumbering great powers, propagating new norms and transforming international society in the process.

Alex Wendt famously envisaged three different types of international society, each of which fulfilled the criterion of being "international" and "anarchical" in the sense of encompassing separate, politically distinctive states that were not united under a world government, yet nonetheless exhibited sufficient variety as to require explanations that could not simply resort to pointing at the absence of world government. Named for different liberal political theorists, these different international societies ranged from the deep suspicion and competitive hostility of a Hobbesian international society, through wary cooperation based on mutual self-interest (Lockean society), to mutual reciprocity and community (Kantian society).[14] These different kinds of society operated in different parts of the world, with the implication that one could be folded into the other, as with the expansion of the EU and NATO into the lands of the former Warsaw Pact. In the words of Richard Ned Lebow, "The post-war transformation of Germany, Japan and the Soviet Union and more recently of South Africa and the countries of Eastern Europe suggest that international society, especially Western regional society, is thicker than previously imagined."[15] Constructivism was, in short, the theory of post-Cold War regime change, and was explicitly cast in such revolutionary terms by Alexander Wendt.[16]

In light of the resurgent authoritarianism and nationalism growing indigenously in the formerly "captive nations" of the old Eastern Bloc, the corruption and economic failure of multiple African National Congress governments in South Africa, the apparent resilience of authoritarian great powers such as China and Russia, and the rise of would-be authoritarian great powers such as Iran, Turkey and Saudi Arabia, these supposed historic successes would need to be rethought. Perhaps the transformative power of international society has been gravely over-estimated – Lebow himself left the question open. More to the point, what was it about the intellectual structure of constructivist theories that lent itself to the latter-day utopianism of liberal order? This can partly be explained by how constructivists envisaged the relationship between political interests and state identity: they collapsed interests into identity, and reasoned that the transformation of identity would in turn transform interests, allowing for the political convergence of otherwise hostile actors.[17]

Carr likened the utopians of his day to the proverbial alchemists who sought to transmute base matter such as lead into noble metals such as gold.[18] So, too, there is a political alchemy at work in construc-tivism, in the hope that base, narrow and egotistical political interests can be transmuted into new, noble, other-oriented identities. Once in-terests are seen as functions of identity, and identities can be changed, then the old harmony of interests is effectively revived. Once again, in the aftermath of the Cold War political interests can be made to converge. While Wendt restricted his analysis to the inter-state level, many constructivists were willing to go further still, as illustrated by Emmanuel Adler:

> Constructivism shows that even our most enduring institutions
> are based on collective understandings; that they are reified
> structures that were once upon a time conceived *ex nihilo* by
> human consciousness; and that these understandings were
> subsequently diffused and consolidated until they were taken
> for granted ... collective understandings provide people with
> reasons why things are as they are and indications as to how they
> should use their material abilities and power.[19]

As Carr noted of liberal utopianism in his day, so too with constructiv-ism: the wish is very much father to the thought. Here we see Adler not only reviving the liberal notion that all political conflict is essentially misunderstanding, but even the notion that grand political change can be essentially pursued *ex nihilo*.

If international order is in fact a society, and one, moreover, that can be usefully understood in terms of the reciprocity, interaction, flexible identity and affective ties of domestic society, then this can only have the effect of blurring the boundaries of international politics as its own specific domain and dissolving the concepts, behaviour and interaction that are specific to it. The problem in this view lies not only in overestimating the transformative capacity of international society but also in the concept of society itself, which was scaled up to the level of the international order. Importing *sociological* concepts of society into international order displaced the specifically *political* concept of society developed by earlier theorists of the so-called English School, who had also sought to understand international politics in terms of an international society. The English School drew on early modern political theorists to conceptualise the paradox of modern state sovereignty: how could the rivalry and conflict of the international realm which political thinkers used to illustrate the character of the pre-political "state of nature" have failed to yield a state at the international level, as it had at the domestic level?[20] Whether society was possible in the absence of sovereignty was understood in terms of contractarian political thought, all of whose variants – Hobbesian, Lockean, Kantian – preserved the idea of society as an artefact of political will. This meant that international society was understood as an association formed by the political assent of multiple sovereign states that was designed for *self*-government as much as regulating interaction between states. That is, international society not only regulated relations between nations and peoples, but also curbed the extent of any one state's power through the establishment of mutual limits, such as the right to non-interference in each other's internal affairs.

Yet with the constructivist concept of international society, political will became redundant. That, for example, Russia, India, China were sceptical or even hostile to democratisation, Western-financed NGOs and humanitarian intervention was no matter, because society and the actors subsumed within could be entirely reconstituted without requiring the positive assent of political will. Just as the lumbering corporations of the old bricks-and-mortar economy would be outflanked by the nimble start-ups of the networked, platform economy, so too great powers and Third World behemoths would now be outwitted by the nimble norm entrepreneurs to whom the future belonged. Whereas the classical view of international society saw it as something constituted through the consent of sovereign states, thus requiring the political assent and the active cooperation of its constituent actors to function, the constructivist-inspired view saw international society *itself* as having substance, as if it were sufficiently cohesive, substantive and ductile that when it was stretched and remoulded, so too would be its constituents.

Thus, not only were questions of political will and positive cooperation dissolved into the ether of international society, so were basic and fundamental questions of power and hierarchy. This is exemplified in the confident and oblivious pontification about "socialising" post-Soviet Russia and China into the (Western-led) international order, the same way that Germany and Japan had supposedly been "socialised" into (Western-led) international institutions after 1945. This sleight-of-hand omits the fact that Germany and Japan were assimilated to the West after a world war which led to them having their sovereignty curbed through prolonged military occupation, political restructuring and, in the case of Germany, ethnic cleansing, territorial truncation and partition. More to the point and as sharply observed by James Heartfield, socialisation is something adults do to children.[21] That this patronising designation could became a ubiquitous term of art in political science, and be casually applied to China – one of the most populous nations on Earth – indicated just how far basic questions of power had slipped from view in the discussion.

Constructivism and constructivist-inspired IR theorising resulted in conceptual levelling, in which all the institutions and complex structures of world order were collapsed and absorbed into a great, gelatinous morass of "society." International society could be seen as an extension of domestic society, producing a vast interconnected latticework of interdependent identities and reciprocal reflex categories defined by relation to each other. This is described by Lebow, and is worth quoting at length to draw out the logic of the claim:

> In practice, neither the United States nor any other developed country has ever come close to resembling a society of egotistic individuals. Sociopaths aside, the rest of us are embedded in a web of relationships ... that begins with families and personal relationships and extends out to business or professional ones and some mix of social, sporting, civic or religious groups and generally beyond this to ethnic, regional and national identifications. We enter into these relationships, because we find purpose and fulfilment by acting in concert with other people. Relationships and affective ties, obligations and loyalties ... teach us who we

are [...] ... The most compelling proof that the world is not composed of egoistic actors is the behaviour of people who actually separate themselves from all social ties ... We observe the same phenomenon at the international level. From Nazi Germany to North Korea, states that reject world society and seek to become truly autonomous actors have become self-destructive pariahs.[22]

Here we have a broad, flat conception of society unwound from the domestic sphere to be stretched out around the globe, and in which, as in interpersonal relations, being isolated produces individual pathology. There are no distinctive institutional or political structures here, no analytically distinct levels (say, domestic society, nations, international order) with their own specific dynamics; no mysterious depths, hidden structures or unconscious forces at work whose existence may have to be inferred because they are not directly observable. Everything is made of the same elastic substance, an ethereal social connectivity, at once immediate and yet abstract. Yet by substituting the glue of social connectivity for the bonds of formally instantiated, collectively agreed on political will, so too is the vision of international society as collective self-government eroded, with the result that there are no limits, no rules or norms that cannot be changed.

As constructivists absorbed international relations as a whole into the gloop of "society," it was only a few short steps to reforming international order itself into the society of academics, and eventually merely the conceit of academics – international order was thus quite literally "(re)constructed" through conference proceedings, commissions, academic "impact," policy advice, reports for governments and think tanks, etc. Here international society becomes an extension of academic networking events, workshops with NGOs and policy makers to discuss strategies for poverty reduction, gender mainstreaming, disseminating human rights, participating in electoral observation missions, and so on. Although not a constructivist in the Wendtian mode, the conceit of this kind of ultra-malleable theorising was most dramatically embodied in Richard K. Ashley's claim that there is tremendous political power imbued in a theorist's pen.[23] Ashley's intent was critical, to suggest that supposedly scientific orthodoxies of neorealism directly contributed to the militarisation, hegemonic practices and rivalries of international politics. He quite evidently did not mean it to also apply to a world in which post-structural theories were more influential than neorealist ones. Presumably, Ashley meant to reduce the status of the proverbial old white men deliberating on world order in distant world capitals and haughty international congresses. With a stroke of his pen, Ashley also boosted the position of academic theorists, so that, say, poststructural workshops could become the equivalent of the Yalta or Potsdam conferences, at which the fate of nations was decided.

If we are to be consistent with Ashley's theorising, then we must draw out its implications. The political implications of this theorising were perhaps most consistently drawn out by constructivist theorist Karl Rove, who derided analysis from the "reality-based community." "We're an empire now," he said, "and when we act, we create our own reality ... We're history's actors."[24] This statement is usually taken as exemplifying the zenith of imperial hubris following the fall of Baghdad to US forces in 2003. Yet here the Bush administration official Rove is in fact expressing eminently constructivist sentiments: that world order is essentially plastic, that it can be changed at will – that all political interests can be made to converge. This reflected the supersession of sovereignty. The sovereignty of other states was as much a limit on oneself as it was a shield for weaker, newly independent nations. For if there is no sovereign right to non-interference, everything is thereby made a direct, immediate matter of global concern – without sovereign borders, how far we can effect change for the better becomes merely a matter of how far our power can reach. It is a world in which the wish is indeed father to the thought, in which there are no unintended consequences or autonomous dynamics that operate of their own accord, such as, for example, a regional balance of power that will spontaneously recalibrate in favour of Iran if the Iraqi state is pulverised, or the relative erosion of US power at the global level as globalisation leads countries to catch up with the US.

Constructivist theorising paves the path to imperial overstretch. Society, much less international order, is *not* a social construct: a human artefact no doubt, but not a social construct. The proof of this is the fact that the international order has changed much less than we might have expected during the period of constructivist ascendancy in the IR academy and the era of constructivist influence. To suggest the international order *is* a social construct, is to suggest that all social processes are essentially voluntaristic, with the implication that social problems are essentially those of outlooks and identities that need to be transformed, a de facto restoration of the harmony of interests. It is difficult to imagine an IR theory more eminently suited to the era of unipolarity than that of constructivism, when there was no countervailing force to that of US power. Carr noted that utopianism is the typical trait of powerful, expansive, and unified political systems, in which the political good will inevitably be seen as an extension of the moral good. He gave the example of the medieval Catholic Church: "It was only with the break-up of the medieval system that the divergence between political theory and political practice became acute and challenging."[25] Luckily, unipolarity and its various ideologies are far less sinuous and tough than medieval Catholicism, and we are again embarking on a divergence between political theory and political practice.

Critical Utopianism

While constructivism developed across a number of influential theorists, critical IR theory was remarkable in being given such a decisive impetus by a single paper published by a single thinker, the late, great Robert Cox – a paper which has long since assumed the iconic status of being more invoked than read.[26] In particular, Cox drew attention to the situatedness and context of theorising: the castles in the clouds always had foundations in the present, he maintained, however remote, rarefied and elegant those castles might appear. If constructivism had grown to become an influential "third theory" that escaped the old Carrian distinction between liberalism and realism critical theory was more explicitly oppositional. Cox's two most famous moves were, first, to assert that all theory had purpose for some particular actor, and, second, to bifurcate the study of international order into two essential types: what he called problem-solving theory and critical theory. As we shall see, this brilliant conceit had all sorts of inadvertent consequences that would mystify more than clarify.

When Cox claimed that theory is always for someone and with some purpose, his intent was critical; that is, it was an injunction designed to cultivate reflexivity. It was a statement intended to encourage social and political scientists, IR scholars and students, theorists and others, to consider how their ideas are informed by and relate to their context. Cox even took his cue from Carr. Just as Carr saw the vacuous shapes of liberal utopianism given content by the status quo powers of the interbellum (the Anglo-French axis), so too Cox's point about critical theorising was to think about how abstract categories might meld with existing structures of power, inequality and hierarchy. Cox was asking, what would give the theories of his own day traction, content and power? After having introduced the distinction between problem-solving and critical theory, he goes on to say, "The perspectives of different historical periods favour one or the other kind of theory." Most intriguingly, he notes that "Periods of apparent stability or fixity in power relations favour the problem-solving approach. The [first] Cold War was one such period."[27] If we were minded to follow Cox's injunction to reflexivity, then we should ask what the current period of critical hegemony in the discipline of IR tells us about the underlying structure of international order prior to and during our twenty years' crisis.

Unfortunately, Cox's injunction to reflexivity has not been taken up. Instead, in following Cox's call for self-conscious, purpose-driven theorising and his division between critical and problem-solving theory, the typical procedure for the critical scholar and student in IR has been to sonorously invoke the critical/problem-solving distinction, claim to be on the right side of it, and then state their purposes – which are, of course, always good ones. For who has bad purposes? These purposes are of course, support for victims of human rights abuses, overturning the oppression of sexual minorities and women, reforming the global economy, supporting the struggles of marginalised indigenous peoples, and so on. Instead of reflexivity, scholars simply assert normative intent and benign purpose and abstractly cast themselves against the putatively oppressive features of contemporary international politics. To be reflexive means to incant gender, class, race and so on, rather than the harder task of thinking through the connection between *our own* ideas and underlying structures of power and political interest.[28]

Criticising existing scholarship as problem-solving became the easiest mode of drawing a line under previous studies while simultaneously denying other scholars' capacities for reasoned analysis or insight, condemning them in one stroke as hapless dupes of existing systems of power. At the same time, by differentiating critical from problem-solving perspectives, Cox implied that solving problems was a lesser task, thus liberating critical approaches from the need to be committed to concrete efforts at improvement and change.[29] Although Cox can certainly not be blamed for academic tribalism stemming from the so-called paradigm wars, from which IR has yet to recover, his distinction certainly helped to legitimate and moralise these divisions, thereby reinforcing the incipient fissiparous tendencies to methodological and theoretical fragmentation.

To be sure, Cox hedged and qualified this distinction in his paper. "Critical theory," he claimed, "is not unconcerned with the problems of the real world. Its aims are just as practical as those of problem-solving theory, but its ... perspective ... transcends that of the existing order, which problem-solving theory takes as its starting point."[30] When Cox offered this as a critique of Kenneth Waltz's structural realism, Waltz batted Cox aside in a single sentence, happily accepting that he was engaged in a different kind of intellectual enterprise, and therefore not needing to engage any further. In Waltz's words, "The alternative is simply to eschew such theories altogether."[31] This has set the pattern for the development of critical theorising in the discipline – the development of fractured, introverted camps that seek neither compromises nor open engagements with each other. Thus, critical IR theory in all its complex variants would end up tracing the arc of liberal utopianism described by Carr, from soaring aspiration for radical change and improvement, blazing most brightly before it disappears beneath the horizon of the present, to ending up affirming the status quo.

Cox's claims were rooted in a Marxisant political economy, although, as Cox emphasised, his ideas were expressly not Marxist and he himself was self-consciously eclectic.[32] Two streams flowed from this work – a new critical political economy inspired by Antonio Gramsci (discussed below), and a more generic critical theory that retains the vestigial remnants of a moral critique of capitalism. Cox understood his own critical theory to be a manifestation of a more contested world order following the relative supersession of the Cold War during the 1970s, as new economic challenges emanated from West Germany, Japan and France and new structures of international organisation and multilateral forms of international coordination emerged following the economic crises of that decade. If problem-solving theory betokened a stable world and Cox's theory a more unstable one, this should raise a question as to how the critical theories of today have come to flourish in a unipolar world ...

Cox was explicitly historicist, drawing on the great Enlightenment thinker Giambattista Vico to understand the dynamics of historical change. As Cox himself stressed, his critical theory was underpinned by economic crisis and the rise of new forms of international institutions and conflict – the historical structures which he was minded to pay attention to were clearly fluid, contested and open to being re-shaped. Cox himself vested his hopes in the New International Economic Order, the vision promoted by the Non-Aligned Movement through various international fora in the 1970s aiming to alter the terms of trade in their favour and secure technology transfers and development funds. Without Cox's historicism and attention to how ideas are moored in the development of underlying social structures, there is no linkage between desired goals and underlying historic shifts. Thus, the stage is set for the utopian follies identified by Carr, this time of a critical rather than liberal variety. Eviscerated of the content that Cox took from Vico, the grand claims of critical intent and stated purpose would inevitably become empty pieties that could be easily moulded to fit the needs of those in power.

The problem was not simply that Cox's epigones were for the most part worse analysts than he was (although they were), but rather a deeper problem with Cox's own understanding of critical theory – the perennial problem of the absence of an agent of change in critical theory.[33] Cox explicitly eschewed Marxism in favour of Vico's historicism, which meant identifying how structures of world orders were embedded in underlying economic modes of production. This style of analysis meant that world orders were captured in the style of a flash-freeze, and change was shown by contrasting a series of these flash-frozen images of different world orders. As with stop motion animation, the appearance of movement is given by displaying a series of frames in rapid sequence.

Having excised contradiction and historical agency from the picture, Cox was unable to conceptualise a social or political actor whose interest or agency was capable of driving the kind of political change he sought. In the turmoil of the 1970s, Cox could, with many others on the left, hitch his wagon to Third World states that were launching revolutions against colonialism and forging ahead with their plans for industrial development and modernisation, seeking to balance their foreign policies independent of both Washington and Moscow in the Non-Aligned Movement. Yet the Third World economic challenge to the status quo would disintegrate in the midst of the debt crisis of the 1980s, and would be superseded once again by the reassertion of geopolitical rivalry between the US and USSR in the so-called second Cold War of that era, usually dated to the Soviet invasion of Afghanistan in 1979. With the end of the Cold War, the Third World could no longer balance between East and West, and itself ceased to have political meaning. Post-Cold-War critical theorists would thus come to vest their hopes in new agents of change – indeed, they would explicitly turn against the very Third World championed by Cox. Many of the Western-led military interventions of the post-Cold-War era which critical theorists would support and justify, have been directed against some of the stalwarts of Cox's old Third World: Yugoslavia, Indonesia, Libya, Syria.

The new critical theorists' preferred agent of change was not the anti-colonial national liberation front that belonged to the classical paradigm of anti-imperialism but, rather, beleaguered ethnic minorities seeking to carve out international protectorates within the territory of the Third World states in places such as Kosovo, East Timor, South Sudan, and Kurdistan with the military support of NATO and the UN.[34] The logic of support for the weak and vulnerable had the benefit that their powerlessness and marginalisation inflated the scope for theorising about them without political costs, risks or even action; the content, however, was provided by Western power. Whereas Cox's insights came from an era of economic contestation and change, the critical theory of the unipolar era unreflexively espoused a unipolar globalisation that appeared to be levitating politics above the nation state into the ether of global civil society. Thus, with the collapse of the Third World and the emergence of the post-political era of unipolar globalisation, critical theorists would inevitably end up becoming more explicitly utopian: aspiration and theoretical obfuscation would substitute for hopes of change. If critical theory were self-consciously contextualised in the era of unipolar globalisation, the only conclusion would be that it melded with existing structures of power.

Cox pushed IR theorists to consider the hegemonic fit between different ideologies and structures of production. As the post-Cold War and our twenty years' crisis have proved, critical theory was clearly well suited to an era of US predominance. After all, multiple cohorts of students have gone off from their university studies in IR to staff the transnational bureaucracy of NGOs, international organisations, global charities, foreign ministries, global multinationals and consultancies, and doubtless many of them are very well versed in Cox's distinctions, as well as the subsequent feminist and poststructural variants of critical theory. Whatever his intent might have been, Cox helped to open the floodgates to a new kind of utopian thinking. The river of critical scholarship that poured forth had no direction, and its force has been dispersed. The result has been a morass of streams and rivulets pouring away into what have become, unfortunately, various intellectual bogs – poststructuralism, feminism, queer international relations, critical queer international relations, critical international law, queer critical international law, animal cosmopolitanism, and so on, leading to predictable dead ends such as the claim that Islamism is more critical than Eurocentric ideas based around the Westphalian state.[35] Stuck in the mire and surrounded by will-o-the-wisps like these, critical theorists assume that everyone outside their vast soggy plain is a primitive ideologue, hopelessly trapped in fixed assumptions, rigid schemas, and dogmatic attachment to the status quo.

Critical Post-Fordism

A second strand of Cox's influence was to propel the thought of one of the founders of the Italian Communist Party, Antonio Gramsci, into IR.[36] Indeed, Cox's influential essay for the journal *Millennium* is one of the best short overviews of Gramsci's thought in any discipline or field. Cox's interpretation of Gramscianism became the touchstone for those who wished to keep critical theory anchored in a material foundation of production structures rather than reducing his insights upwards into the realm of discourse. Yet, paradoxically, those who wield Cox as an axe to cleave their own projects from existing scholarship and proclaim their critical superiority over mere problem-solvers repeat precisely the sin with which Cox charged problem-solving theory – taking the sphere of production for granted.[37]

The surge of interest in Gramsci in the 1970s allowed Marxists and Marxisant radicals to distance themselves from the legacy of Russian revolutionary leader V.I. Lenin, whose reputation was besmirched by the sinister Soviet cult built around his legacy. Gramsci's martyrdom in a fascist prison made him a more appealing figure, freed from the burdens of wielding political power and all the dilemmas, both moral and political, that flow from that. Gramsci drew on Niccolò Machiavelli in his writings, but paradoxically his own appeal rested on being effectively an (enforced) idealist languishing in prison, in contrast to Lenin, who was not only an enthusiastic realist but also a "practitioner" in addition to being a theorist. So, too, in IR and Critical International Political Economy, Cox helped to dislodge Lenin in favour of Gramsci. What was perverse about this was that Lenin had written extensively and directly about the structure of international political economy, great-power politics, the domestic sources of foreign policy, imperial rivalry, colonisation, revolutionary and anti-imperial revolt, revolutionary foreign policy and national self-determination – all in pointed contrast to Gramsci's opaque, highly metaphorical and fragmented musings from prison. This again was part of Gramsci's hermetic appeal. As a leftist martyr to fascism, Gramsci was sufficiently Marxist for his students and followers to be able to register a vague concern with matters economic. At the same time, Gramsci was also focused on matters that would luckily spare his followers the tedium of having to trawl through statistics on capital export, bank mergers, industrial combination, or, say, the number of *poods* given over to tobacco cultivation in the pre-war Russian Empire. This was the kind of evidence that Lenin preferred to use to back up his arguments, as opposed to the highly stylised genealogies of "post-Fordism" that become de rigeur for Gramscians – sketches that are ultimately closer to a materialist cultural sociology than a Marxist political economy. Thus Gramsci became academics' and IR academics' favourite Marxist.

Cox's channelling of Gramsci into IR carried with it several problems that would sow the seeds for the new post-Cold-War utopianism of critical theory. The first was the concern with consensual forms of power. Gramsci famously borrowed the image of power as a centaur from Machiavelli; power was part man, part beast – part reasoned justification, part brute force. Gramsci's innovation was, according to Cox, to transplant the Bolshevik understanding of their own political leadership in revolutionary Russia to explain the continued leadership of the bourgeoisie in Western Europe – a resilience that was too strong to be explained purely by reference to brute force. Thus, the consent of the governed classes required an explanation at least as much as state power did. This was the famed "hegemony"; how to explain the hegemony of established elites over the subaltern classes?

Yet, in what would become an endless disciplinary disquisition on various forms of "hegemony," critical theorists assumed, with Cox, that Marx's theory was effectively addressed to the question of crude power – hence the need for them to analyse the more subtle, consensual aspects of power with which people seemed to assent to their own domination. Yet this was to reckon without Marx's actual theory, which was a critique of political economy – expressly an attempt to account for and locate domination in the process of capitalist production that occurred beyond the realm of state power. In short, in its original and most systematically developed form, Marx's explanation never had recourse to direct forms of power to begin with. Structured around the spontaneous mystification of commodity fetishism, Marx's critique of political economy does not require consent to be understood as the supplement to brute coercion, for, as Marx stresses, the wage-labour relationship that is at the core of capitalist society is *already* formally consensual, even fair. The deflection to "consent" as the *explanandum* for critical theory conveniently and carefully avoided the sophistication and subtlety of the Marxian critique of political economy. The mystery for critical scientific investigation no longer lay in explaining how domination is rooted in the act of equivalent exchange that occurs in the process of production, but rather in attempting to explain how people are duped into blithely accepting political orders that critical theorists happen to find distasteful.

Gramsci's second error was to locate the source of this ineffable "consent" in civil society. "In the West there was a proper relation between state and civil society and when the state trembled a study structure of civil society was at once revealed," he claimed.[38] From this flowed the assumption that, because bourgeois hegemony was "firmly entrenched" in civil society, the state had thus been left to the rule of other classes, such as the aristocracy, as long as these political rulers recognised "the hegemonic structures of civil society as the basic limits of their political action."[39] This assessment, derived from the putative study of nineteenth-century capitalism, underestimated the fact that, as Marx made clear in his *Eighteenth Brumaire*, the bourgeois renunciation of political power in that period was a historic *retreat* by the bourgeoisie, representing the abandonment of its own historical mission. Thus, it was the class that had been dedicated to overthrowing the militarised absolutist state in favour of freedom and commerce that had allowed the modern, nationalist and authoritarian state to re-emerge in its midst, complete with a new generation of populist, militaristic and nationalist leaders. By deflecting to civil society, the political failures of the bourgeoisie were obscured, the new authoritarian state was taken for granted – one might even say "naturalised" – and with it the question of political rule and state power was deferred in favour of the attritional work of constructing counter-hegemony in civil society. Cultural influence substitutes for political power. This became the template for the failures of Italian communism in the Cold War: great films, great theoretical journals, great style – but no power – or at least, power only as long as they clung to the coat tails of the Christian Democrats.[40]

Cox sought explicitly to turn away from the political-military inter-relations of states, to focus instead on the more diffuse and abstract "social forces" emanating through world order and crystallising in vari-ous forms of social movement – an insight that Cox himself attributed to his role as a civil servant for the International Labour Organisation.[41] Projected onto the global stage, Gramscian critical theory helped avoid the basic questions of state power in favour of devising abstract paral-lelograms of social forces cutting across nation-states, and then imagin-ing how critical theorists' preferred movements might be coordinated. Alliances were grandly proclaimed at world social forums and social movements insinuated themselves into international organisations.[42] Movementism has long since been a tributary feeding the river of left populism – the Workers' Party in Brazil, Podemos in Spain, Momen-tum in Jeremy Corbyn's Labour Party, Syriza in Greece.[43] These are parties that all, ironically enough, show themselves to repeat the same problems in their inability to deal with the specific form of political power embedded in the EU, on which more in the next chapter. To be sure, Cox was not the only radical theorist to eschew questions of polit-ical power in favour of movementism – the same has been done by the likes of Michael Hardt and Antonio Negri; the theorist of the Zapatista insurgency, John Holloway; and the theorist of the Occupy movement, David Graeber, among others. Nonetheless, Cox reinforced it and but-tressed it with analyses that were far more concrete, evidenced and su-perior to the likes of, say, Hardt and Negri. The ultimate political and theoretical payoff was, however, the same.

Much like Carl von Clausewitz and Sun Tzu are taught in manage-ment and business courses to make management consultants and bankers feel like statesmen and generals, so too theories of Gramscian hegemony have allowed multiple generations of radical academics to fancy themselves "organic intellectuals," grandly devising strategies for uniting radical social movements to construct a counter-hegemony, bristling with the gratifyingly martial jargon of Gramscianism – "war of movement," "war of position," as well as the metaphorical trenches, fortresses, earthworks and ditches of civil society – all of which (luckily) turned out to be so many synonyms for the ivory tower in the lexicon of the critical theorist. In practice, theorising hegemony and especially "counter-hegemony" has obviated the need for theorising both political power or principles; these can be brushed aside in favour of thinking through the convolutions and contortions of alliance-mongering among social movements. The self-flattering notion of "organic intellectuals" that was adopted from Gramsci – that is, intellectuals nestled in social constituencies – was the conceptual means of collapsing the distance required for articulating interests through representative politics and leadership. As the problem of consent is essentially cast as one of the poor and vulnerable being gullible to the mysterious cultural wiles of "the bourgeoisie," so too the discussions of "constructing" "counter-hegemony" degenerate into opportunistic attempts to assemble the pieces of the radical movement jigsaw that will, in reality, never fit together in anything resembling a coherent picture. Politically, it amounts to little more than working out how to dupe potential supporters into being "hegemonised" rather than considering the harder questions of how people's interests may be given political form, organisation, and representation. After all, people may want political leadership, but who wishes to be hegemonised? Counter-hegemony resolved itself as counter-summitry for those with the resources and time to traipse from one elite summit to the next to protest on the outside across the 1990s and early 2000s.

Ironically, the global social movements succeeded in capturing the commanding heights of international organisation just as radical right populists began to capture state power. The year that saw Trump win the White House also saw the IMF publish an article denouncing neoliberalism.[44] "Counter-hegemony" had finally triumphed. Yet, while it was the alter-globalisation movement that had pioneered global opposition to neoliberalism, it was the Trumpian neo-mercantilist coalition of capitalists who would implement the political programme, to the consternation of critical theorists. Fair trade, not free trade, was the slogan of the anti-globalisers and now, nearly twenty years after US trade unionists dumped cheap Brazilian steel into the harbour of Seattle during the anti-globalisation protests of that year, it was President Trump who, in 2018, imposed tariffs of 25 per cent on steel imports. It was the critical theorists who provided the ideological battering rams against neoliberal globalisation, but it was the radical right populists who would storm the citadel – or rather, amble through the gates that the Gramscian critical theorists and the anti-globalisers had already shattered. As Mark Fisher aptly observed, the anti-globalisation movement ultimately provided little more than "carnivalesque back-ground noise to capitalist realism."[45] Having deferred the question of political power while they were busy in the "trenches" of civil society, the critical theorists were unhinged with horror when the archetypal neoliberal candidate, Hillary Clinton, was defeated by Donald Trump. By winning hegemony in transnational civil society, the academy and social movements, the critical theorists and movementists had evaded questions of political power and representation, thereby mirroring the failure of the liberal middle classes in the mid-nineteenth century in their willingness to abdicate questions of political power.

The failure to deal with political power inevitably meant that critical theorists would adapt around it and be shaped by it. Nowhere is this more tragically evident than in Brazil, once the global heartland of "alter-globalisation." For all the grand declamations against global capitalism, ultimately the anti-globalisation movement functioned to provide legitimacy for the neoliberal *Partido dos Trabalhadores* (Work-ers' Party [PT]), which was ignominiously ousted from power in a de facto "soft coup" mounted by the Brazilian elite in 2016. The canny former leader of the PT and ex-president, Luiz Ignácio "Lula" da Silva, gave the anti-globalisation radicals a sandpit to play in when he al-lowed the World Social Forum to be hosted in the southern Brazilian city of Porto Alegre, a bastion of radical municipal government. Writ-ing in the *New Left Review*, anti-globalisation theorist Hardt hailed the forum as nothing less than a "new Bandung," invoking the great inter-state congress from the heroic era of Third World liberation that had once enamoured Cox.[46] In effect, however, the World Social Forum provided little more than radical ornamentation for the PT government while Lula loyally kowtowed to international financial institutions. In 2004, the year after the last World Social Forum was held in Porto Alegre, Lula despatched Brazilian troops to Haiti to act as part of the UN occupation of Port-au-Prince. At the time of writing, the viceroys that Lula once sent to Haiti now act as senior cabinet figures in the militarised government of his radical right successor, the current presi-dent of Brazil, Jair Bolsonaro.[47] The troops and police forces that Lula sent to occupy Haiti are being redeployed at home to wage war on the favelas from whence he once drew his electoral support, while he was imprisoned on corruption charges, a de facto political prisoner.[48] Critical theorists meanwhile impotently flail at Bolsonaro from afar, misguidedly calling him the "Trump of the Tropics."[49]

What is ironic about all this is it was Cox himself who predicted it. Writing in the aftermath of the 1970s, Cox mapped out three possible scenarios as emergent outcomes of the era. He labelled these three scenarios hegemonic, non-hegemonic and counter-hegemonic. The "hegemonic" scenario was in effect the globalised world order of the thirty-year period from 1979 to 2008, and was associated with the political leadership of US president Ronald Reagan and British prime minister Margaret Thatcher. It was indeed characterised, as Cox had expected, by the internationalisation of production, monetary policies designed to combat inflation and maintain exchange rate stability at the expense of employment and real wages. It was also centred around core North Atlantic economies and based on new forms of labour market regimentation and hierarchy.[50] At the opposite end of the spectrum was Cox's most desired, and, by his own admission, less likely outcome, the "counter-hegemonic scenario." Cox saw this scenario as involving the overthrow of the core-periphery relationship embedded in the international order that built on the model of the New International Economic Order of the 1970s. According to Cox, building this scenario would require presenting "a coherent view of an alternative world order"[51] built around a state-based class, "mostly petty bourgeois in origin combining party, bureaucratic and military personnel whose radicalism would need to be sustained from below in the form of a genuine populism" – a frank (and frankly shocking) endorsement of Third World left-Bonapartism, perhaps best exemplified by the Peruvian junta of 1968 to 1980, and more recently by the regime of Hugo Chávez in Venezuela.[52]

Most interesting from our historical vantage point is Cox's second possible outcome, "a non-hegemonic world structure of conflicting power centres." Cox predicted this would necessitate the ascendancy in several core countries of neo-mercantilist coalitions which would link national capital and established labour organisations, both of which would want to opt out of arrangements designed to promote international capital and instead organise their own power and welfare on a national or sphere of influence basis.[53] This new coalition would be explicitly counter-monetarist, disparaging "monetarism for subordinating national welfare to external forces and for sharing an illusory faith in the markets." In a follow-up essay, Cox went further, envisaging "a broad alliance of the disadvantaged against the sector of capital and labour which find common ground in international production and the monopoly-liberal world order," complete with post-Keynesian and neo-mercantilist policies.[54]

There are important elements missing from Cox's picture here – China's having emerged as a major capitalist economy and exporting power; the implosion of the command economies of the Eastern Bloc; a de facto counter-monetarist regime of low interest rates created by those very same independent central banks envisioned by the monetarists themselves; and a more ragged working class, its independent civic and political organisations having been chewed up during the preceding era of neoliberal hegemony. Notwithstanding these distortions in the picture, what Cox is describing here decades in advance is very clearly a Trumpian non-hegemony, right down to the deracinated blue collar voters of the northeast "rust belt" switching their votes from the Democrats to Trump in 2016.

Doubtless, many critical theorists would blanch at the thought of Donald Trump as Gramsci's "Modern Prince," with his trade tsar Robert Lighthizer and former political strategist Steve Bannon occupying the critical theorists' coveted roles as the Prince's advisers and theorists of counter-hegemony. Yet resistance to the accuracy of this picture would only expose how much Coxian critical theorists are self-deceiving utopian liberals. The critical theorists who claim Cox's legacy and have built successful academic careers critiquing global hegemony around the world at major international conferences now fiercely assail the "non-hegemonic world" predicted by Cox, while they desperately cling to the "hegemonic world order" that is crumbling around them. They have shown themselves oblivious not only to Cox's predictions but also to his injunction that critical theory needs to be "conscious of its own relativity" based on "a broader time perspective" and that it needs to "to avoid undertaking theorising for the purposes of systemic equilibrium and reproduction."[55] This is precisely what contemporary critical IR has not done.

Thus the problems of critical theory and constructivism are indeed theoretical ones, and they have been exacerbated by unipolar globalisation. What is it about unipolarity that dulls the edge of social scientific investigation and theorisation? It is significantly linked to the structure of international order. The fundamental lack of political contestation – ideological and geopolitical – means that there is no vantage point to be gained by seeking independence between poles. Moreover, unipolar globalisation undercuts the search for underlying effects or structural causation. Everything can be read off the surface, either as an effect of globalisation or American empire, and every countervailing ebb of the tide or countercurrent can be hysterically swollen into "resistance," whether that be crude Third World Bonapartists like Venezuelan leader Nicolás Maduro, Hezbollah guerrillas, anti-globalisation activists or kooky art exhibitions. This failure to account for the relationship between theorising and the underlying social division, structures and distribution of political power inevitably means that the concepts, theories, and intellectual frameworks are free-floating and amorphous, and can be easily be made to meld with the needs and interests of power.

By contrast, in a politically competitive world, or at least a world in transition, analysts should be under greater pressure to consider how their frameworks, theories, concepts and ideas relate to different power centres. Do they choose a side, or do they need to navigate between them? Either way, they are forced to consider how their ideas express and meld with underlying power structures.

Conclusion

When Robert Cox died in late 2018, many IR scholars paid gushing tribute to the extent of his influence while ignoring the power of his foresight – despite the fact that he had predicted that very same non-hegemonic international order that was prompting so much consternation among his supposed followers.[56] Cox even hypothesised that a financial crisis was "the most likely way in which the existing world order could begin to collapse."[57] Today, the claim to be critical is so common in international studies as to be banal. It is not much different in intellectual terms than the management-speak of claiming to be "thinking outside the box." Just as anyone who claims to be thinking outside the box is in fact doing precisely the opposite the very moment they invoke that tired metaphor, so too with "critical" IR theory – a claim to be critical is usually a signal that all critical thought petrified a long time ago. Once Cox introduced this distinction, all hitherto existing scholarship could now, with a stroke, be cast as limited, narrow, orthodox, ideological, simply by being indicted for being problem-solving. Those claiming to be critical morally boosted themselves as daring, innovative, heterodox. Thus the prefix "critical" turned out to be even more tendentious than Carr's claim to be "realist."

Just as Carr had thereby pre-empted all opposition to his arguments as unrealistic by default, so too with Cox: all other approaches could now be cast as uncritical by default.[58] We could even say that if Carr's distinction between realism and liberalism was the intellectual bifurcation that originated in the multipolar world of the inter-war era and would become the organising intellectual framework for the bipolar one, so Cox's bifurcation between problem-solving and critical theory was the intellectual bifurcation for the unipolar world that originated in the Cold War-era bipolar world. In other words, it turned out that both critical and problem-solving approaches were contained within the single system of unipolarity.

Yet, far from seeing himself as the ur-type of our contemporary critical scholars, Cox claimed to be a conservative. For him, this entailed "a commitment to a certain sense of right and equity for the underdog and a suspicion of the most recently established wealth and power – a pre-capitalist, Jacobite, anti-Whig conservatism."[59] His keen sense of historical self-awareness and honesty speaks to the superiority of his insight and theory. His latter-day Jacobitism was perhaps best expressed in his wager on the Third World as a counter-hegemonic global force, for both Jacobitism and Third Worldism were doomed lost causes if ever there were any. His followers by contrast are merely postmodern Whigs, forlornly attached to a degraded liberalism, with their instinctual conservatism now exposed as they wistfully hark back to the lost world of 2016 before Trump and Brexit. In any case, all of Cox's hoped-for counter-hegemonic "historic blocs" have crumpled, including the alter-globalisation movement.[60] "Theory is always for someone and for some purpose," Cox famously averred.[61] Critical theory turned out to be "for" a sharp-elbowed new academic elite seeking to oust a previous generation, while its "purpose" was to provide legitimation for the neoliberal world order, not least in intellectually corroding the idea of state sovereignty in which political will could be exercised independently of a global market. Yet if critical theorising is no longer reflexive, then what is its purpose?

Similarly, Alex Wendt had the advantage of being able to offer a plausible if ultimately unconvincing account of the burst of political transformation at the end of the Cold War. Subsequently, however, the neo-utopian impulses of these theories accommodated themselves to the new power structure of a unipolar international order. In light of the emerging new centres of Cox's "non-hegemonic" world, it is interesting to revisit the predictions of Cox and Wendt's old intellectual sparring partner and self-confessed "problem solver," Kenneth Waltz, who had expected multipolarity to emerge in the early aftermath of the Cold War. Despite this failed forecast, revisiting Waltzian predictions is a fascinating exercise. Waltz notoriously welcomed the spread of nuclear weapons, thinking that their deterrent power would help to preserve international peace – an outlook that would seem to be vindicated in the chaos of Libya, which renounced its nuclear armaments programme and was subjected to a devastating NATO air campaign in short order. Nuclear-armed North Korea by contrast enjoys senior summitry with the post-hegemonic Prince himself, Donald Trump.

Just as the dissolution of the Warsaw Pact helped to liberate Eastern Europe, Waltz expected the dissolution of NATO to "liberate" Western Europe, forcing the Europeans to assume political responsibility for their own continent – what he saw as an "exhilarating" prospect.[62] It is difficult to imagine any critical theorist advocating for anything as radical as the dissolution of NATO, let alone calling for the "liberation" of Western Europe, or any decolonial theorist calling for the nuclear proliferation that would actually help to guarantee the political independence of the post-colonial nations that they supposedly cherish. What is an argument for nuclear proliferation in the formerly colonial world, when compared to the apparently more radical debate over dead white men on a university curriculum? Indeed, the only leader putting political pressure on NATO is US president Donald Trump. Critical theorists prefer to provide gender mainstreaming advice in NATO workshops, or, perhaps if more constructively inclined, helping to "socialise" the backwards East Europeans into the mysteries of Western liberal democracy. Such is the conservatism of contemporary critical theory.

3 Washed up on the Shores of Eutopia

Introduction

On 4 March 2019, the French president Emmanuel Macron published a letter in twenty-four languages across the European Union (EU) directly addressing himself to its many citizens in advance of the Union-wide elections to the European Parliament in May that year.[1] In the letter, President Macron called for renewing the EU project. He did this by denouncing Brexit as built on lies, against which he asserted the continuing vitality and necessity of the EU, with a range of sweeping proposals for renewal. Nothing vindicates the EU, it seems, as much as the effort to leave it. The tortuous difficulty, long-term economic costs and political turmoil of extricating the rickety old British union from the newer continental one has seemed to help solidify the latter, as indicated in opinion polls across the continent. A YouGov Eurotrack poll published in April 2019 found that in countries across the Union, support for remaining in the EU had been significantly strengthened since 2016. Yet the same poll found that when asked about their views of the future of the EU, respondents were deeply pessimistic.[2] This single poll contains within it perhaps the central contradictions of the EU: that it appears inescapable and yet at the same time is seen as unviable.

Brexit has been variously denounced either as a neo-imperial fantasy or as demonstrating the limits of autarky and sovereignty, expressing a wilful isolationism and refusal to engage the outside world. It is thus widely seen to exemplify political unrealism in world affairs today, as Britain's aging voters are beguiled by the mirage of pristine isolation, imperial nostalgia and racial *ressentiment*. Adjudicating the origins and fate of Brexit is beyond the scope of this chapter. Instead what I want to argue here is that at least as many if not more fantastical premises are required to imagine that the EU can endure as a viable long-term political system. The EU is quite evidently a liberal utopian project, and to that end it can be usefully studied using the critical lenses provided by E.H. Carr – especially in identifying the storied harmony of interests that is required to sustain the fantasy of successful European integration. Thus, of all manifestations of the new forms of liberal utopianism in international affairs today, nowhere is it more entrenched and insidious than with regard to the EU.[3] Eighty years after Carr charged liberal utopians with bringing Europe to the brink of war with their legalistic dogma, institutional rigidity and political infantilism, Europe is once again flirting with destructive forces, not only for having stumbled into a proxy war with Russia in Ukraine, but also for having created debt-colonies throughout the Eurozone and for its the ruthless efforts to suppress democracy to preserve the Union, as seen in Greece, Ireland and Italy through technocratic usurpation, repeat referendums and external curbs on the fiscal autonomy of elected governments.

The EU has all the prototypical rigidity and brittleness of last utopias. Francis Fukuyama's much maligned and misunderstood end of history thesis has often been caricatured as expressing the foolish naivety of liberal hubris and American exceptionalism at the end of the Cold War. Yet, as Fukuyama himself stressed, it was always the European Union that exemplified his paradigm of historical completeness; he even bor-

rowed the EU's earlier identity to describe the post-historical process –
believing that "Common Marketization" would engulf and eventually
overwhelm the classical power struggles of international politics.[4] This,
I aver, is the politics of Eutopianism.

I take the phrase Eutopianism from Professors Kalypso Nicolaïdis
and Robert Howse in a paper that they co-authored for the *Journal of
Common Market Studies* in 2002. Their intent was positive, as they were
writing in the flush of enthusiasm in advance of EU enlargement eastwards to absorb the former Eastern Bloc. Nicolaïdis and Howse were
happy to use the designation "Eutopia" unironically, seeing in the EU a
vision for a concrete constitutional order that could be globalised and
act as a political counterweight to the soulless neoliberal globalisation
embodied in the World Trade Organization (WTO). They explicitly
define Eutopianism against traditional utopianism, characterising the
latter as "normativity that demands absolute principles of substantive
justice, regardless of context, or [that] fetishises any particular set of
policy instruments and institutions."[5] Notwithstanding the absence
of any vision of substantive justice at the core of the EU project, I argue
in this chapter that this definition of utopianism matches quite closely
the behaviour and ideology of latter-day Eutopia. The paradigm of liberal utopianism that I propose here manifests in the determination to
preserve an anti-ideological order that cannot accommodate political
and economic change, with the result that it collapses into a nihilistic
attempt to freeze the status quo.

Eutopianism is also the last and perhaps the most formidable bastion of Eurocentrism in international politics – it is the concrete political manifestation of this particularist ideology. The reason we know
that the EU is the last (highest?) stage of Eurocentrism is because, first,
it is quite literally Eurocentric, and second, because it is the Eurocentric conception of world politics that all the traditional opponents
of Eurocentrism fiercely defend – notably, decolonial thinkers and
critical race theorists, for whom (ironically) a world without powerful
pan-European political structures seems quite literally inconceivable.[6]
The abiding strength of Eurocentrism is reflected in the persistent inability to imagine a world without the EU as an expansionist political project with world-historic significance. Eutopianism is thus the
missing category in the taxonomy of Eurocentric politics developed by
John M. Hobson in his study of this phenomenon.[7] While the critical
theorists strain mightily to purge all lingering traces of Eurocentrism

from IR theory, they have been content to see it grow in political and institutional strength in Brussels and Strasbourg. Whatever their theoretical claims, the bitter depths of these thinkers' political Eurocentrism can be measured by the shrill intensity with which they inveigh against Brexit as a racist, neo-imperial project, in defiance of the polling evidence of British social attitudes and with studied silence on actually existing European neo-imperialism in the Balkans and Libya. This studied ignorance of Eutopian empire today – especially in Europe itself – is unsurprising, as decolonial and post-colonial critics hark back to a purely maritime idea of empire as something that happens far away and overseas, in places such as the Caribbean, Africa and Asia. That so many of the nations of Eastern, Central and Southeastern Europe were themselves imperial subjects does not concern the Anglocentric, decolonial critics of Brexit. Intricate "genealogies" of white racial supremacy are constructed to help explain that the Brexit vote perpetuates British imperialism, while the mass murder of African and Arab migrants and refugees, left to drown in the Mediterranean, is ignored. This is the actual politics of decolonial theory. Eurocentrism in theory is denounced, while actually existing Eurocentrism – the European Central Bank (ECB), the European Commission, the European Council, the European Court of Justice (ECJ) – are all defended as part of the necessary ramparts against ... a resurgent Eurocentric racism. Having renounced the universalism of the European Enlightenment, decolonial and critical race theorists settle instead for the ugly particularism of the EU, mired in its xenophobic conspiracy theories of Russian subversion on the one hand, while it repulses refugees from its shores on the other.

In the old-fashioned lore of IR, it was Carr's supposed impaling of the liberal idealists in 1939 that marked the intellectual victory of hard-headed realism over the starry-eyed, feeble-minded utopians of world politics. Yet it is difficult to think of a policy that institutionalises the flaws of liberal utopianism as much as the euro.[8] Eighty years after the supposed triumph of Carrian realism, it is remarkable how closely the Eurozone resembles the European ideal of one of Carr's bitterest critics, the great neoliberal thinker F.A. von Hayek. The European Union itself resembles Hayek's collaborator Ludwig von Mises's vision of European federation. Carr curtly dismissed these two thinkers in 1947 as "old fashioned economists."[9] Indeed, historian Quinn Slobodian has noted how much the neoliberals of the post-war era such as Hayek and Mises were the "Lost Causers" of the international order of the interbellum, embedded in the League of Nations, as they continued to fight for its political vision long after it had been swept away.[10] Yet today they could certainly not be dismissed as breezily as Carr dismissed them in the late 1940s. Just as much as the Kosovo War embodied the belated triumph of Carr's liberal utopian foe Lord David Davies, so too the EU and the Eurozone signal the extent to which any vestigial Carrian insight has been evacuated from contemporary European politics. IR theorists themselves have thus renounced their contribution to the debate on Europe. These are the political and intellectual costs of having renounced the legacy of the "first great debate" in IR. Indeed, in IR today Carr is even claimed by critical theorists as having been in the vanguard of Eutopian politics, a forerunner of political supranationalism. This is a view that misconstrues Carr's thought and evacuates some of his key insights, as we shall see below. Before reconsidering Carr's supposed Eutopianism, however, let us consider some of the many facets of actually existing Eutopianism today.

Financing Eutopia

For all the brutality of Eutopianism in maintaining the walls of Fortress Europe, perhaps the most long-lasting damage to international order will be that inflicted by the Eurozone.[11] I made the case in chapter 1 that the start of our twenty years' crisis can be dated to 1999, due first to the Kosovo War, but second, and more significantly, to the fateful unification of multiple national currencies in Western Europe into a single new currency – the euro.

Yet the contradictions of the Eurozone may yet prove to be more damaging to world order over the long run than the era of permanent war seen with liberal hegemony. The economic costs of the Eurozone have been striking, as seen in the economic calamity inflicted on Greece, the shocking regression in Italy, the enormous youth unemployment across the southern tier of the Union, the devastation inflicted on smaller economies such as Ireland and the Baltic states, with westward mass migration compounding the demographic collapse of Eastern Europe.[12] Carr was famously hostile to abstract solutions that did not match concrete, actually existing conditions. Yet so grandiloquently ambitious is the Eurozone that it verges on a caricature of utopian folly that hardly merits being subjected to the subtle manipulations of Carr's dialectic. A continent-spanning Procrustean framework that binds together vastly divergent economies with the fantastical promise of eventual economic convergence, the Eurozone embodies a conceit that would outrank some of the most absurd utopian follies of the last two centuries. In many ways, the utopianism of the Eurozone is worse than the liberal utopianism of the League, or indeed the gold standard, to which the euro has been accurately compared.[13] As Carr discussed in his *International Relations between the Two World Wars*, countries came off the gold standard during the interbellum as a way of managing their balance of payments problems, with some success.[14] For all the folly of the League, the allure of its technocracy dissolved away as it failed to fit the scale of growing political problems. "Once it came to be believed in League circles," Carr observed, "that salvation could be found in a perfect card-index, and that the unruly flow of international politics could be canalised into a set of logically impregnable abstract formulae ... the end of the League as an effective political instrument was in sight."[15] In other words, the more the League resorted to technocracy, the more it consigned itself to irrelevance. Although we have long since reached and gone beyond this point with the Eurozone, abstract formulae continue to govern European politics: centrally controlled interest and exchange rates have proved more rigid than mere League habits of mind, or even, indeed, the gold standard itself. Thus Carr shared much of the Keynesian critique of the interbellum and disparaged the notion that liberal pieties on "self-determination" could resolve deeply entrenched problems of economic integration.

Yet – and here we must deviate from Carr – this is precisely the lesson of the Eurozone; namely, that successful economies necessitate self-government, which in turn subsumes self-determination. This is true not only in having independent national currencies that can fluctuate to absorb economic shocks, but also by considering the impact of the euro on national economic structures. Take the paradigmatic case of Italy. As the work of Lucio Baccaro suggests, the strategy of external constraint, by which Italian technocrats sought to transform Italy's economy, has stunted productivity growth.[16] In seeking to outflank domestic actors by embedding Italy in the Eurozone, the currency union has locked in policies of market liberalisation and privatisation that impede reaping economies of scale, technological innovation and the substitution of capital for labour that was a traditional engine of Italian growth in the post-war era. In short, political self-determination is now once again a precondition for sustained economic improvement.

The case against the Eurozone can also be made in political terms.[17] As at long last, serious critical studies of the Eurozone are emerging, here I only wish to draw out some of the political and strategic implications of this Eutopian currency union.[18] The political and social costs of extracting nations from the iron cage of the Eurozone is likely to be much more difficult, costly and tense than anything witnessed with Brexit, which is after all only a secession from the EU's political institutions, Britain being fortunate enough to retain its own currency. As already mentioned, Hayek, one of Carr's bitterest foes, envisaged a common currency and central bank to dilute and curb the remit of state intervention in the economies of the interbellum.[19] Yet as Carr noted, liberal utopianism could not help but camouflage power politics; this was a condition of its conceit. So, too, the Eurozone is just as thoroughly saturated with power political considerations. As noted by Adam Tooze, the basic questions of the European macroeconomy "are political all the way down." [20] As the euro emerged from the French hope to contain Germany after the end of the Cold War, the end result has been a de facto new German empire in Europe that has expanded beyond its traditional sphere of influence in *Mittel-Europa* to the shores of the Mediterranean

Unsurprisingly, President Macron's "Letter to Europe" of March 2019 passes over the Eurozone in silence, aside from the comment that the Eurozone helped spare Europe from the ravages of the financial crisis – a comment that would be risible were it not so brazenly delusional.[21] The Eurozone gives the lie to all the other proposed adornments of Eutopia, such as Macron's proposed "European Climate Bank," "European Internal Security Council" or "European Intervention Initiative." German defence minister Annegret Kramp-Karrenbaue responded to Macron's letter by offering the French president a "European aircraft carrier."[22] This was effectively an offer to subsidise the French military, most of whose resources are devoured by maintaining the *force de frappe*. As consolation for German economic domination that will never be turned into a German-dominated superstate, the French would instead receive the most redundant and overrated weapons systems available today as a payoff to spare the blushes of France's fading imperial glory (with its single carrier the *Charles de Gaulle*) and as compensation for the fact that Germany will simply not turn the Eurozone into a fully fledged fiscal union to underpin French debts.[23] Even a glittering bauble such as an aircraft carrier comes at a cost however: Ms Kramp-Karrenbaue called Macron's sub-Gaullist bluff on greater European cooperation when she asked that in return for the aircraft carrier, France relinquish its veto-wielding permanent seat on the UN Security Council in favour of a jointly-held EU seat.[24] Macron has since responded by recourse to the French diplomacy of the interbellum – seeking to counter-balance Germany by flattering the states of Eastern Europe and reaching out to Russia. In a much-vaunted interview with the *Economist* in late 2019 Macron proposed a grand strategic rapprochement with Russian leader Vladimir Putin – this after having stoked Russophobic conspiracy theories over Russian support for Macron's domestic rivals.[25] Whether or not the Euro-carrier eventually gets built or not or whether Macron's rapprochement with Moscow materialises, is moot. The point is rather that it is this flimsy structure of national jockeying and petty compromises between leading European states that constitutes the foundation on which the whole tottering structure of Eutopian economics is built.

Even here, there are limits. The German economic machine, sputtering across 2019 and built on many years of wage repression, will strain to pay for actually existing Eutopia, let alone Macron's super-charged Eutopianism.[26] The irrationality of the German economic machine can be seen in its exorbitant export surpluses, more akin to a developing country rather than an advanced economy, locking Germany into a competition with industrialising countries that it cannot win.[27] Once Germany's demographic decline, vast social security payments for its aging population and its internal regional development funds are factored in, compounded with the fact that Germany will have to pay more to the EU to compensate for Britain's withdrawal – not to mention the deeply rooted management malpractice and corruption exposed during the Volkswagen "diesel dupe" scandal of 2015 – German economic domination then looks less solid over the medium to long term. Once the Eurozone dissolves, German exports could be as much as 20 per cent more expensive if valued in Deutschmarks rather than euros.[28] The subsidy provided by the Eurozone to German exporters has shrouded the underlying problems of the German economic machine for some time.[29] As Wolfgang Münchau points out, mighty German industry has failed to make the transition to a twenty-first century of electric batteries and artificial intelligence, with "Mercedes ... still selling the fuel-driven car Karl Benz first patented in 1886."[30] Despite this, German Euroscepticism is only likely to grow, as Germany's position is squeezed by the new Latin axis in the Eurozone, comprising

French president Macron, Italian prime minister Giuseppe Conte and Christine Lagarde at the helm of the European Central Bank – all of whom will push Germany to save less and spend more on behalf of Europe as a whole.[31]

Eutopianism is thus always most evident with the Eurozone, and in particular with the flights of fancy that Eutopians adopt when they seek to mount any honest assessment of their own project. It has become a commonplace among some scholars to compare the travails of the Eurozone to the struggle over union debt and national banks between Thomas Jefferson and Alexander Hamilton in the early days of the American republic, the vindication of which is seen to lie in the solidity of the US today.[32] Beset by challenges on all sides, the last reflex of Eutopianism is, paradoxically, indeed the telos of all classical utopianism. All the difficulties of the present can be superseded from the imagined vantage point of the future. The current era is nothing more than the federal state of the future retroactively struggling to cohere itself in our present: we suffer on behalf of the future; the working lives of whole generations have already been sacrificed to this ideal, with the astonishing rates of youth unemployment seen across the southern EU. Thus, some of the most technical, complex, rigorous and supposedly "scientific" studies of the Eurozone rely on magical thinking like this, perched on the stilts of the most ridiculous historical analogies. Comparisons to the American federation are also chilling, because what these Eutopians are effectively promising us with this comparison is a great continental war of national unification yet to come. After all, it was the 1861–65 Civil War – still the bloodiest war ever fought by the US – that resolved the multilevel governance problems of the young American republic, decisively establishing that sovereignty lay with the union and not with its constituent states.

It is a common Eutopian hope that Britain withdrawing from the EU will help to deepen the continental Union, as Britain was always an advocate of broadening rather than deepening the organisation. Yet what is likely to happen is that France's power will probably be at least temporarily boosted, because Germany had relied on Britain as a counterweight to France.[33] Just as the Eurozone struggles to suppress Franco-German rivalry, so too the EU today is itself a geopolitical artefact of power. Just as US hegemony and the establishment of NATO were the preconditions for the early phases of European integration in the first half of the Cold War, so the era of unipolarity has permitted the simultaneous deepening *and* broadening of the EU, allowing EU elites to avoid this traditional trade-off in their political calculations. Thus in the era of unipolarity we have seen both institutional consolidation within the core of the EU *and* expansion eastwards and southwards. Unipolarity also facilitated the accelerated decompression of traditionally centralised nation-states, with regional and sub-national autonomy becoming more prevalent throughout the Union as the stakes of secession were reduced in a transformed European geopolitical space. This Eutopia of sub-national units, autonomous regions, devolved territories and provincial so-called nations which strings together the Bretons and Cornish with the Welsh and Catalans, would also meet its geopolitical limits when the EU slouched into a proxy war with Russia in Ukraine, redounding to new geopolitical rivalries in Europe itself, across Belorussia, Serbia, North Macedonia, Montenegro and Bosnia-Herzegovina. Having relentlessly expanded to the borders of Russia itself, anything that is seen as threatening to Eunity is now derided by the Eutopians as so many Putinite fifth columns.

Thus Catalans, Brexiters, supporters of the League in Italy and *Front National* / National Rally voters in France are all seen alternately as agents or dupes of Moscow – aside from Scottish nationalists of course, who serve as a useful thorn in the flesh of Brexit secessionism. The results of policies of regional autonomy that have been pursued for decades by Brussels are now blamed on Moscow. What has changed is not so much Russian policy as the geopolitical conditions around which Eutopian policy was designed: Russia has enjoyed a limited recovery from the nadir of the 1990s, and the EU has overextended itself in Eastern Europe, whereas the US is shifting its attention westwards, to the Asia-Pacific. It is this global context that has led to the Eutopian scorn heaped on the Catalans, as well as the unstinting political support offered by Brussels in 2018 to the central government in Madrid in its heavy-handed and thuggish response to would-be Catalan secessionists. It is also this global context that explains why the project of Eutopian expansion is over, as indicated in October 2019 when French president Emmanuel Macron vetoed bids by Albania and North Macedonia to join the EU.

Not only does traditional power politics condition Eutopianism, it itself expresses a kind of utopianism of power. The EU is cast as a peace project, growing out of the catastrophic experience of the Second World War. This "learning from war" thesis is intended to flatter Europe's political elites, endowing them with the glamour of historical wisdom and tragedy. Yet if it were true, the EU would not then have stumbled into a proxy war with Russia in Ukraine, nor would its member states have enthusiastically supported pulverising the Libyan state with the NATO bombing campaign in 2011. Moreover, the EU as a "peace project" is also what has given European nations the right to wage war in the name of human rights. This sentiment was perhaps best expressed by Joschka Fischer, the German foreign minister during the Kosovo War and a leading light of the Green Party. Fisher was instrumental in reconciling his hitherto pacifist party to war, on the grounds that Germany's experience of fascism justified a war against the supposedly fascist regime of Serbian leader Slobodan Milošević.[34]

Beneath sentiments such as these is the longing for the EU to be a *Weltmacht* as clearly expressed in Macron's letter and the far-ranging and controversial interview he granted to the *Economist* in November 2019. Here, the EU is envisaged as a global competitor equal with China, Russia and the US, with its own spheres of influence in its own "near abroad" – the Balkans, the Levant and North Africa. Most grandly, of course, this resolves in the new Macronist visions for Africa, with France in the lead – a sinister postmodern revitalisation of "Eurafrica" in which the whole continent will serve as a vast imperial backyard, providing the cheap, youthful labour and plentiful resources needed to boost the ailing EU to fulfill Macron's dream of global hegemony. Eutopians sneer at the delusions of a post-Brexit "Global Britain" while consistently hoping to spur EU military cooperation to ever grander heights, dreaming of an EU legion to police the Sahel and rapprochement with Russia to extend Eutopian influence to the borders of China itself.

The congenital strategic weakness of the EU has the added benefit that it promises an endless stream of academic debate on the EU's "soft," "civilian," or "normative" power and its status as a "regulatory superpower." These conceits fulfill multiple needs at once: lamenting the lack of EU military power provides a normative gloss on the actuality of neo-imperialism in the Balkans and Africa. It also provides self-exculpation in the case of its having helped to spark civil war in Ukraine, as well, in the last instance, wistful self-flattery in which academics and Eurocrats can devise grand schemes for EU common defence and security, safe in the knowledge that they are all preordained to fail – failures which can in turn be gratifyingly blamed on the self-absorption, national egotism and consumerist materialism of Europe's voters, who fail to rouse themselves from their stupor to serve the grand visions of their political masters and social superiors. Thus is the beautiful soul of Eutopianism preserved.

Ultimately, the EU is an attempt to prolong Europe's time on the international stage, seeking to stave off what the post-colonial historian Dipesh Chakrabarty called the "provincialisation" of Europe: its diminution in world-history. It is this prospect that especially fills decolonial thinkers and critical theorists with dread, because they know that with European decline, their supposedly radical schemes for improved world order will have less heft. Nowhere is this more evident than in the assertions of radical and critical academics in Britain, who insist that transnationalism is the path to redemption because they fear that in a weakened post-Brexit Britain, they will be left out of discussions on say, the Women, Peace and Security agenda at the United Nations, human rights in Tibet, gender mainstreaming in African police forces, or whatever – it is after all their own status that matters more to them than Africa or Tibet.[35] This Eutopianism belongs to the tradition of what Mark Mazower called imperial internationalism. This tradition encompassed schemes from the first half of the twentieth century for sublimating the transnational infrastructure of the British Empire into new forms of international cooperation and world government, thereby allowing these imperial internationalists to circumvent the selfishness of their national working classes, who were weighing down these grand schemes by seeking to assert their interests within Britain itself.[36] The imperial internationalists of the early twentieth century – comprising Fabians as well as League enthusiasts such as the South African statesman Jan Smuts – strongly overlapped with the liberal utopians castigated by Carr (e.g., the theorist of world government, Leonard Woolf, belonged to both camps). So too today, the EU provides a new kind of transnational imperial polity that enables Eutopians and latter-day Fabians of IR to crank themselves out of the messiness of national democratic politics and clamber onto the world historic stage, where they imagine they can hector Africans and jostle as peers at least with the Russians and Turks if not quite the Americans and Chinese.

The EU makes Europeans once again the centre of the world. Its endless introspective debates about constitutional reform and relations between its various convoluted branches of governance and multiple presidencies can be held aloft as grand experiments in new forms of transnational rule. Its tedious, endless regulatory discussions about slapping around American monopolies, Chinese tech giants and Russian energy companies make it relevant in Washington, Beijing and Moscow, where, it is hoped, EU trade and competition lawyers can bore their opponents into submission through their mastery of arcane regulations. The fear that without the EU Europe will inevitably slide into nationalism and world war not only overlooks the EU's complicity in the Ukrainian civil war, but also betokens the nostalgic conceit that Europe remains the centre of the world, the cockpit of world-historic rivalry in which the fate of the planet will be decided. Just as the struggle for power in Europe led to world war in the first half of the twentieth century and made Europe the epicentre of the Cold War, so today Europeans burbling about the EU as a "peace project" have not accustomed themselves to the fact that the world's centre of gravity has shifted to the Asia-Pacific and it is there that the fate of the world will be decided. The truth is that without the EU, Europe will slide to where it belongs – into world-historic provincialisation.

Writing in 1939, Carr endorsed the sentiments of the British prime minister of the day, Neville Chamberlain, who had earlier remarked, on Japanese atrocities in the Sino-Japanese War, that if "it was not that China was so far away, and that the scenes which were taking place there were so remote from our everyday consciousness, the sentiment of it, horror and indignation which would be aroused by a full observation of those events might drive [the British] people to courses which perhaps they had never yet contemplated."[37] Europeans will have to accept sentiments such as these in the twenty-first century, but from the other end of the telescope. That is, they will have to consider how ethnic conflicts and secession in places such as Kosovo, Catalonia, Abkhazia and Transnistria, or protests in Syntagma Square or indeed Paris itself, will seem at the remote, far end of the 7,000 kilometers of train track and road that constitute the New Silk Road traversing Eurasia. In the map of the world that hangs in Shanghai's Pudong Airport, only four European cities are marked – Paris, London, Berlin and Duisburg. Of the four, Duisburg, hitherto a backwater in the German rustbelt, is the biggest on the map: it is the western terminus of the Belt and Road.[38]

That the EU continually lends itself to liberal utopianism from every point on the political spectrum merits a book length study in itself. Here, a few points will have to suffice. The concatenation of utopias associated with the EU reflects, I believe, the structural malformation of the EU as a polity. That is, anyone, irrespective of their political or national background, ideological proclivity or intellectual inclination, can seize upon any EU agency or institution they like and then happily extrapolate to their desired future. From the EU Parliament, one infers a thriving, vibrant continental democracy in the future in which ordinary people and not just Jean Monnet professors will actually care about European elections. From the Eurozone, one extrapolates to a true future federation, in which a minimal, stripped back super-state oversees an integrated continental market that pulses with freely flowing factors of production – labour, capital, goods and services – to produce a harmony of interests through fabled economic convergence. From the Commission, another looks forward to a regulatory future in which a highly trained cadre of virtuous, technocratic experts primly protect our consumer rights from predatory US and Chinese corporations. From the ECJ, another can look forward to a grand and intricate cosmopolitan legal order on a continental scale, in which everyone's individual human rights are safeguarded at a higher level than merely that of the nation, safely insulated from the tyranny of the majority within states. From the EU peacekeeping missions and eastern expansion, another fondly conjures up the image of a benevolent neo-medieval empire, with its various institutional strands intermeshed across its overlapping structures of authority, finally achieving that chimerical dream of a peaceful imperialism. From the Single Market and Customs Union, another imagines a future socialist continent in which redistribution, nationalisation and public spending can all be mounted on a lavish continental scale and in which the Germans and Dutch will happily endure tax for the sake of Greeks and Italians. Others still see the opportunity for a new "civilisation-state" in which the faded Christian West is united to preserve its ebbing strength from the challenges of a populous and febrile Islamic world on Europe's borders.

Thus radical right populists, neo-Hegelians, cosmopolitans, globalists, federalists, Marxists, critical theorists, Critical Theorists, Hayekian neoliberals, technocratic centrists, liberals, old social democrats, old fashioned Christian Democrats, conservatives, human rights enthusiasts – all survey the irregular range of EU institutions and seize upon one peak, imagining in the hazy purple distance that it is the tallest one. Yet the jagged crags of the EU political system betoken its structural and congenital malformation, its lack of any centripetal coherence or overall rationality.[39] Its malformation is not a defect that will be overcome in the fullness of time, but is, rather, the necessary condition of its functioning. The fact that the achievement of any particular goal is always deferred to some distant, hazy point in the future is the tell-tale shimmer that gives away utopian thinking. To understand this requires us to consider the historical development of the European state over the last century.

Utopian Carrism

This brings us to a consideration of Carr's views on supranationalism. As indicated above, even Carr himself conceded to this utopian impulse to refashion a Europe of the imagination, prompting post-Cold-War critical theorists to claim a "critical" and even a "cosmopolitan Carr."[40] Instead of the blithe and chilly doyen of realism ruthlessly puncturing political illusion, we are instead given Carr the visionary who supposedly foresaw the necessity of supranationalism and the need to enlarge political community beyond the nation-state.[41] Although Carr certainly argued that utopianism was needed to counterbalance the aridity of realism, it is inattention to the context in which Carr was writing that has allowed him to be anachronistically mistaken for an IR critical theorist *avant la lettre*.

Carr's views of a new "welfare internationalism" that would extend economic planning and redistribution across nations was developed in the context of the Second World War. Here Carr saw the supersession of Wilsonian nationalism in the diasporic multinationalism of the white Dominions of the British Empire rallying to the mother country in her hour of need and in the multiethnic composition of the US and Soviet armies.[42] In the joint global military commands of the Allied forces, Carr looked to a world of "pooled" rather than League-style collective security. Meanwhile, de facto global economic planning was undertaken by United Nations relief agencies and Allied ministries to coordinate a global war effort across multiple theatres while simultaneously mounting relief operations to war zones. However, to elide Carr's analysis of wartime supranationalism with the EU and its precursors – the European Coal and Steel Community was only formed in 1952, seven years after the end of the war – would be to drastically misconstrue his views *and* miss his important insights into the development of European politics.

For Carr, US-UK wartime planning was of a piece with Nazi coordination of the European economy after Hitler's conquests and the emergence of the Soviet command economy in Eurasia.[43] All of them indicated, in Carr's mind, the supersession of nineteenth-century liberal economy, and liberal order more generally. Indeed, Carr even held that Soviet multiethnic and multinational federalism offered an appealing model that could bridge the extremes of vacuous League-style world order schemes on the one hand, and the disarray of small upstart independent nations on the other.[44]

Contrast this with the critical theorists of Carr's day – that is, actual members of the early Frankfurt School in Germany and the US – who were horrified by the dissolution of bourgeois individuality in atavistic fascist collectivism, and saw the more centralised, authoritarian state capitalism of their era as a mark of capitalist decline and regression rather than a welcome harbinger of progressive change.[45] Carr's contempt for nineteenth-century liberalism extended to contempt for the national hopes of Central and Eastern Europe. Content before the war to write off the small European nations of the interbellum to German domination, he was equally content to see them fall under Soviet domination after the war.[46]

Inattentive to this context, critical theorists today are, unsurprisingly, also inattentive to their own context and how it conditions their approach to Carr. In the age of unipolar globalisation and cruise missile liberalism, conjuring with the spirit of Carr allowed critical theorists to advance their own cosmopolitan politics under the cover of his hard-headed realist pragmatism. Thus, cosmopolitan thinkers were all too happy to adopt Carr's contempt for the sovereignty of small nations when they endorsed the humanitarian wars of the 1990s and early 2000s, while Carr's invocation of "welfare internationalism" allowed them forlornly to register their opposition to neoliberal economics. Yet, ironically, that element of Carr's thought ruled out by critical theorist Andrew Linklater as simply foreign and alien to our time – Carr's hostility to economic laissez faire liberalism – has been revived by none other than Donald Trump. On the other hand, Carr's putative call for "new forms of political community" and "post-exclusionary forms of political organization" – tropes which Linklater judged as the "most significant and enduring" element of Carr's thought – are precisely those elements that now seem most imperilled by the travails of the EU.[47]

The post-Cold War remoulding of Carr into a Eutopian critical theorist thus does him a disservice. Not only does it treat him in a decidedly uncritical fashion, it also cuts away some of his most penetrating insights into the formation of post-war European politics – namely, the fact that he rooted the historic necessity of European supranationalism not in some proto-cosmopolitan yearning for harmony, but in the de facto unification of the continent enacted by Hitler during the world war.[48] This last point is somewhat mysteriously underplayed by the critical theorists who champion Carr as a forerunner of the EU.[49] Yet Carr's insight about Hitler laying the ground for European unification is entirely correct. That it would be guiltily buried by those claiming Carr for the EU only shows the miasma into which the discipline has sunk.[50]

Carr saw Hitler's early victories less as testimony to Nazi power as much as to the weakness and brittleness of the liberal nation-state – a theme we shall return to in the conclusion. Not only were the Wilsonian states of inter-war Eastern and Central Europe all variously overrun, dismembered, annexed, conquered or subjugated alternately by Germany and the USSR across 1939 and 1945, but even the archetypal nation-state, France itself, fell to Nazi conquest in May 1940. While Carr saw pro-fascist secession and "quislingism" as predictable in the newly manufactured Versailles states of Yugoslavia and Czechoslovakia, the "widespread 'collaboration' in [France,] the European country with the oldest and most deeply rooted national tradition of all was a new and startling development."[51] Carr, with his usual perspicacity, could see that Nazi victories were not in fact "wholly explicable in terms of brute force" and they were "difficult to reconcile with the picture of an age of unbridled nationalism."[52] Carr's observations are worth drawing out here at length:

> Ten or twelve million foreign workers in German factories, factories in occupied countries working under high pressure on war production, substantial contingents of a dozen foreign nationalities embodied in the German armies, the extensive recruitment of foreigners not only for the rank and file, but for the officer corps [and] *Waffen S.S.* [...] Hitler's victories in 1940 and 1941 ... [were] at once a symptom and a cause of the decline of nationalism ... plausibility must be accorded to a shrewd comment penned at the peak of German power in Europe that "Hitler's successes are basically rooted, not in his extreme nationalism, but on the contrary in his shrewd judgement of the decay of nationalism among his neighbours.[53]

It was here that the foundations of Eutopian unity were laid.[54] Having swept away the rickety superstructure of Europe's nation-states, it was the belated effort of Hitler's armaments minister Albert Speer to rationalise the German war economy on a continental scale in the militarisation and slave labour policies gestured at by Carr above, that in turn laid the infrastructure for a post-national, post-war European economy through continental planning and cooperation among Western Europe's industrial elites. This was underpinned by the fortuitous circumstances of Nazi occupation, which allowed for the suppression of borders, unions, workers and wages.[55]

The bourgeois will to self-rule in the form of independent nationhood – the principle around which the bourgeoisie had restructured Europe in the nineteenth century – crumpled in the face of working class revolt in the interbellum before it collapsed under Panzer tanks. Collaborationist political and industrial elites disgraced themselves in cooperating with the Nazis, and thus it was left to the partisans and resistance fighters – frequently communists and socialists – to restore national honour.[56] Having already renounced national honour and sovereignty in favour of prostrating themselves before Nazism, the post-war elites of Western Europe were happy to dissolve it away again in new forms of post-war international cooperation.

Carr's insight into the Nazi origins of post-war European unity could even be pressed into service today to help explain the Brexit vote of 2016. Inasmuch as there remains a withered, vestigial commitment to the idea of self-government within Britain's contemporary political elite – whether recalled under Churchill or Atlee – it can be partly explained by the *absence* of Nazi occupation and a collaborationist regime that would have shattered elite authority and will to self-government, as it did elsewhere in Europe.[57] In any case, these vestigial growths are so withered that they have already shown themselves barely sufficient to sustain Britain's secession from the Union.

Yet by the same measure that Carr diagnosed the weakness of the nation-state, he overestimated the alternatives to it. Carr saw that fascism would not be able to unite Europe, and he was also right that economies of scale, industrial concentration, technology and new means of transport all militated for superseding the nation-state. Yet he missed the fact that practical alternatives to the nation-state had been eliminated, not only in the barbarism of Nazi empire-building, but also by the Soviet Union itself – that political order that Carr consistently overestimated throughout the twentieth century. It was, after all, Stalin's putatively realist creed of "socialism in one country" that had relegitimated the very idea of nationhood. After the war, Stalin insisted that the wartime anti-fascist national liberation struggles were scaled up into collaboration with post-war bourgeois governments, while in Britain he mandated a "super-patriotic," anti-American line for Britain's communist intellectuals and trade unionists.[58] The development of Stalin's policies, which would end up renewing the decidedly unrealistic nation-state, was described by Carr in two books that no IR scholar ever reads, and in which Carr recounts the decline of communist internationalism: namely *Twilight of the Comintern 1930–1935* and *The Comintern and Spanish Civil War*.[59]

The Third or Communist International (Comintern), was originally conceived as a global party structure of which even the Soviet state itself was merely a subsidiary, temporary appendage. The Comintern was dissolved by Stalin in 1943, signalling his commitment to the wartime alliance of the United Nations and marking the USSR's emergence as a geopolitical keystone of the post-war order. With this, Moscow renounced any lingering commitment to a post-national and stateless future as embodied in the red globalism of Lenin's early Soviet state.[60] Carr was curtly dismissive of Lenin's ostensibly idealist policies of proletarian internationalism, missing the fact that their eclipse by Stalin's more nationalist-infused realism would resolve itself in the recreation of that same nation-state that Carr so despised. Thus, what Carr reckoned as a nineteenth-century liberal anachronism was preserved across the twentieth century in Wilsonian and later Stalinist aspic.[61]

As we can see, a critical engagement with Carr yields more insight than simply pressing him into the service of Eutopia. Carr's Eutopianism, such as it was, was based on his vision of a world divided among compact, autarkic power blocs based on planned economies – a decidedly anti-cosmopolitan vision, and one that would be at odds with the neoliberal economic structures of the EU. It was also an era in which Europe was still the centre of the world. Part of Carr's rationale for a post-war "European Planning Authority" was that it would immediately also be a global planning authority, by encompassing Europe's overseas imperial possessions.[62] To ignore the mid-twentieth century, post-war context within which Carr framed his views of European integration – not to mention his admiration for Soviet "integration" in Eastern Europe – speaks to critical theorists' obliviousness to the conditions of European integration since 1992. So what are these conditions, and how do they frame contemporary understandings of European integration?

From Utopianism to Eutopianism: The New "Harmony of Interests"

A common misconception about the League of Nations and inter-war liberal idealism is that it was born of despair at the horrors of the First World War, a misconception that would have been corrected by reading E.H. Carr.[63] The League was born of a tremendous surge of liberal triumphalism and hope, the personal popularity of Woodrow Wilson and Wilsonian ideals, with the Great War widely believed to have marked the triumph of liberal democracy over the militarism and monarchical despotism of the Central Powers. No less important, as Carr makes clear, the League was born of the massification of politics and its spilling over into the realm of international affairs. As Carr noted, the Great War not only made it impossible to leave war to professional soldiers, it also made it impossible to leave international politics to professional diplomats.[64] It was no accident that the League was designed in a self-consciously parliamentary fashion, with a bicameral structure replicating the institutions of representative democracy at the international level: mass oversight and accountability was to be offered not only at the national but also at the international level. Carr sees in the popular agitation against the secret treaties of the pre-war period the first symptom of the demand for popularising international politics. Indeed, he went further, claiming that it was this political agitation that directly heralded "the birth of a new science" of international politics.[65]

There has since been a counter-revolution in all these domains – attempts to constrain mass politics, to deflect public scrutiny and diminish public accountability in international life. The Anglo-American powers recognised the force of Carr's claims on the massification of war by switching from a labour-intensive to a capital- and technology-intensive mode of fighting: air and naval power supplemented with special forces and proxies (first and foremost among them, the Soviet army on the Eastern Front). In this way the Anglo-American powers sought to curb the political disruption of mass mobilisation. Analogously, there has been a counter-revolution in diplomacy.[66] The ramifications of this counter-revolution have impacted not only political practice, but also as we have seen political science and theory. The diplomatic historian and theorist G.R. Berridge dates this process back to the 1960s, which saw the revival of the old, highly professionalised pre-war diplomacy in new guises.[67]

Berridge sees this in the procedure of informal consultation in international discussion as hollowing out the significance of voting in international fora and thereby substituting for the old, pre-Wilsonian "secret discussion." Berridge also draws attention to the rise of a new diplomatic infrastructure that bypasses resident missions – "the spine of the old diplomacy" – in initiatives such as the G8 forum and serial summitry. Berridge stresses how serial summitry in particular incarnates the old diplomacy in a new era of mass politics. It does this by helping to institutionalise close inter-elite connections that deflate "excessive public expectations" by "fostering a sense that the encounters are routine."[68] As Berridge stresses, "continuity of personal contact" was always "the central procedural principle of the old diplomacy understood by all of its theorists from Cardinal Richelieu in the seventeenth century to Harold Nicolson in the twentieth."[69]

I want to argue here that, unlike the liberal utopianism of the interbellum that arises out of the hope and optimism of the early post-war period, Eutopianism was born of the pessimism of the counter-revolution in international affairs and diplomacy, in this case taken to its greatest extreme. Not only does Eutopian politics insulate intra-European diplomacy from the incursions of mass politics, it also rolls over into demassifying politics *within states themselves*. This is the transition from nation-states to member states, in which a national government is plugged into a continental network of permanent inter-elite connections, resulting in "government by diplomacy" that achieves its zenith in the European Council. Frequently misconstrued as a democratic body by virtue of being constituted by elected national representatives, the Council in fact transplants decision making from the domestic sphere to the international sphere: its authority derives from its transnational character, not from electors in Poland, Italy, Spain, or wherever.

James Heartfield laid the foundations for the theory of member statehood in his chapter on the EU in the 2007 collection of scholarly essays *Politics without Sovereignty: A Critique of Contemporary International Relations*. Here he argued that the EU and its various precursors grew in inverse proportion to the hollowing out of mass democracy and party politics at the national level. Christopher J. Bickerton fleshed out and

extended this insight by showing that this was not just a negative process, characterised by the dissolution and absence of democratic politics, but that it had also resulted in a substantive transformation – the
transformation from the classical European nation-state to the European member-state. Thus, member-statehood did not involve merely
donning the external trappings of membership, but also embodied an
intensive *internal* transformation of the political and economic structures of the state, as we shall see in greater detail below. The great insight of member-state theory is that it enables us to see that the growth
of the EU was not a structure bolted onto states from the outside,
but the external manifestation of a wide-ranging *internal* transformation. The beauty and effectiveness of member-state theory is that it
can simultaneously and consistently account for multiple phenomena
of European transnational politics while also allowing us to snap the
contrastive manacles of supranationalism on the one hand and inter-
governmentalism on the other. Otherwise all political developments
are forced to be seen either as trending towards a federalised European
super-state, or else as nothing more than ornaments for national interests and old-fashioned diplomacy.

Member-state theory thus complements wider trends in political
science in which the erosion of mass democracy by new techniques
of technocratic government has become prevalent, ranging from the
compression of the ideological spectrum through the "cartelisation" of
political parties to the independence of central banks.[70] In the period
of significant political turmoil to come, member-state theory provides
the conceptual razor to slice through the many paradoxes of European
politics and Eutopian delusions.

From Nation-State to Member-State

Yanis Varoufakis, the finance minister of Greece during the Greek
debt crisis of 2015, subtitled his account of his time in power, *Adults in
the Room*, with *My Battle with Europe's Deep Establishment*.[71] It is a nice
turn of phrase, evocative of the idea of a "deep state." Originally used
to apply to the strongly nationalist and authoritarian Turkish officer
class which consistently curbed Turkish democratic politics over the
twentieth century, this term of art from Middle Eastern-area studies
has now been globalised. In a conspiratorially minded age, it is used
to invoke mysterious and deeply embedded structures of state power

that manipulate the theatre of democratic politics. Varoufakis said "establishment," not state, as it's clear that there is no European state. The implication is that the task of democratic politics is to reach into this establishment, expose it and turn it inside out.

Yet there is no deep inner core to penetrate. As Bickerton stresses, the Eurocracy in Brussels itself is tiny, smaller than many national-level government departments.[72] Member-state theory makes clear that it is a serious conceptual error to think of the European transnational state or establishment as "deep." The political problem of the EU remains internal to the national state itself. This requires us to shift the conceptual dimensions and perspective of our analysis. Instead of a vertical analysis – looking downwards into the mysterious depths to identify the structures of the "Euro deep state" – we have to shift to the horizontal level, and focus instead on how transformed European states relate to each other through the EU. That is, it requires us to consider the way in which "national interest" is embedded in and (re)articulated at the transnational level.[73] What is important to realise is that the fictive "harmony of interests" castigated by Carr and invoked by utopians in the interbellum to conjure up common interests where there were none, has actually *been constructed and institutionalised* at a pan-European, inter-elite level. However, this has only been possible because it is detached from the process of interest-formation at the national level – in other words, insulated from public accountability and pressure.

This new harmony of interests is sustained by being embedded in a complex "Eurocracy" of multiple, transnational regulatory agencies and subnational actors, with powerful "PermReps" – permanent representatives of member-states – forming the spine of the process. All processes of decision making – the "trilogues" between the Council of the EU, the Commission and Parliament, and the processes of so-called co-decisions – involve aligning national representatives and coordinating across and within EU institutions. That the Euro-elite succeed in constructing a harmony of interests is indicated in the prevalence of so-called early agreements – unsurprisingly, given that power is exercised behind closed doors and embedded in the very institutional forms and procedures of the EU itself. These are bodies such as Coreper, the European Council, the Eurogroup – all of which are deeply secretive.[74] At the national level, these processes are associated with increasing presidentialism and empowered executives distanced from the electorate and in which legitimacy is based more on "output" than "input" – i.e., legitimacy derives from political achievements rather than the democratic integrity of the process by which decisions are reached and enacted. In addition to empowered executives, we see judicialisation and agentification, in which state bureaucracy is increasingly privatised and regulatory monitoring roles are assigned to independent agencies. The process is especially pronounced in the UK, which helps explain the hysteria that gripped Britain's elite during the years since the invocation of Article 50 to leave the European Union. The hollowed-out British state is incapable of functioning as a ruling body once it is excised from the transnational mesh of the EU. The overall result has been the decoupling of politics from policy. As discussed by Vivian Schmidt, we have policy without politics at the supranational level and politics without policy at the national level, mirroring the political divide between liberal technocratic centrists and populist nationalists, respectively.[75]

Cast in terms of political theory, member statehood amounts to supranational constitutionalisation, encasing democratic politics in rigid forms to curb and constrain popular will as with, say, the Electoral College or Supreme Court in the US. In the EU, these equivalent agencies have the added benefit of not only being reified within archaic constitutional structures, they are even elevated above the nation itself. As every American schoolchild is taught, the Supreme Court in the US was envisaged as part of an integrated system of "checks and balances." The European Court of Justice, however, reigns supreme over the laws of many nations with no counterbalancing agency: the European Parliament cannot check it; indeed, the parliament cannot even initiate legislation. It is a parliament whose Potemkin status is so flimsy and obvious that the *Duma* of the Tsars would seem a vigorous organ of popular democratic energy by comparison. As Richard Tuck argues, constitutionalisation impedes political change. The EU, however, scales this up a notch further, because the constitutions are treaties, and changing the treaties requires coordinated manoeuvring between all member states to effect constitutional change within the Union.[76]

Thus, the advantage of member-state theory is that it allows for a more unified integration of these diverse domestic and international-level phenomena, while also allowing us to see the EU as a unitary political system in itself. Member-state theory helps explain the growing rigidity of national political systems – the growth of technocracy – without any corresponding growth in the size or scale of supranational bureaucracy. At the international level, it helps explain the enhanced inter-governmentalism within the EU at the expense of the supra-national Commission – a balance of power that does not, however, manifest itself in greater democratic empowerment at the national level. In particular, member-state theory explains the phenomenon of how the EU can *amplify* the capacity of states *without* empowering cit-izenry at the national level. This is the notorious discussion over the benefits of "pooling sovereignty" – say, for instance, in providing a united front in global trade negotiations with other major global econ-omies, or enabling greater defence cooperation across borders. Yet the empowering of the EU through the pooling of sovereignty does not empower the EU at the ballot box, where it has tended consistently to lose in recent times, as with the French (2005), Dutch (2005, 2016), Irish (2008) and British (2016) referenda.

For cosmopolitans and Eutopians, amplifying national power by coordinating with other states justifies the EU in transcending the nation-state. Yet this amplification of state power – external sover-eignty – is contingent on widespread popular disenfranchisement – the hollowing out of internal sovereignty. Member-state theory helps ex-plain how this trade-off has been accomplished, and why the supposed benefits of pooled sovereignty do not translate into what popular sovereignty is supposed to provide – popular control. Carr dispar-aged the "harmony of interests" as utopian in a world of mass politics. Eutopians have proved him right, as they have built their empire by insulating the process of interest-formation from mass politics, insu-lating it from popular control by boosting it out of reach, to the trans-national level. The costs of this strategy are now evident: as domestic political systems begin to fragment and realign, the foundations of transnational politics begin to crumble. Indeed, even taken on its own terms, although Eutopian politics can harmonise interests, it comes at the expense not only of popular politics but also of limiting the range of policy options available to states – most notably, the Eurozone pre-vents national currency devaluation that would help countries absorb the shock of economic crises and adjustments.[77]

In his sweeping survey of European integration, Perry Anderson struggles with the European Union, and he ricochets between various makeshift frameworks before he eventually settles on classifying the EU as an ideal Hayekian transnational state – small, rigid, pared down to the bare constitutional essentials and tightly organised around market discipline.[78] What this misses is that this supposed transnational state is the outgrowth of member states, and must be seen as continuous with them. At some level, differentiating the member-state from the supranational structure is redundant: the member-state exists as a continuum of political space from the national to the supranational, but, contra Anderson, it is as large, cumbersome and crude as Leviathans always are, especially in the Eurozone. It was the Stability and Growth Pact, which limits public spending across the Union, that prompted the *gilets jaunes* revolt in France in late 2018, as national-level green fuel taxes squeezed peri- and ex-urban working-class and lower-middle-class citizens dependent on their cars to get to work. Macron's regime of rubber bullet liberalism in France is enforcing the writ of the EU through the form of the member state. The most important political battles against the EU are always those that are internal to states themselves.

Finally, the clear implication of member-state theory is that there will be no European state, super-, supra- or otherwise. In its grappling with absolutism, the bourgeoisie either established or upgraded representative institutions to imprint its political and commercial interests onto the pre-existing structures of monarchical and absolutist states. These representative structures were in turn subsequently democratised and expanded as women, the plebeian orders and the propertyless were incorporated into the political nation. Carr called this process of political massification the "socialisation" of the nation – its extension from the propertied classes to the masses.[79] By contrast, the EU was constructed as part of the *flight* from mass politics in the latter part of the twentieth century. The express purpose of the EU is and always has been to outflank and subvert representative institutions. National-level representative institutions will not be replicated at the transnational/European level because that would simply replicate the problem – the incursions of mass politics – that these institutions were designed to avoid in the first place.

Conclusion

At the end of Carr's most Eutopian work, *Conditions of Peace*, he noted, "The old world is dead. The future lies with those who can resolutely turn their back on it and face the new world with understanding, courage and imagination."[80] Today's Eutopians have singularly failed to rise to this challenge, as they doggedly cling to the failing Eurozone and its technocratic appendages.

From the perspective of Brexit Britain over the last three years, what has been most interesting to observe is the *volte face* in the intelligentsia's attitudes towards the EU. Prior to Brexit, it would have been fair to say that to any outside observer, the EU was little loved. The democratic deficit was universally acknowledged, the cumbersome processes in which the EU bureaucracy worked well known, the foibles of EU foreign policy widely accepted. It was accepted that it was a deeply flawed institution, and intelligent debate about its shortcomings was possible. In the space of a few months surrounding the Brexit referendum, the EU transmogrified into the last best hope of humanity. Stephen Hix portentously declaimed that with Brexit, we were turning our backs on a resplendent peak of human development "in our small corner of the planet."[81] Eutopianism thus has many of the characteristics of what Samuel Moyn described as "last utopian" thinking – the final utopia built at the end and on the ruins of all the other utopias, to which we cling to all the more tenaciously because it is presented as a modest, post-utopian achievement. Life outside the EU is inconceivable for many of the liberal professional classes, producing the most remarkable derangement throughout the intelligentsia. Mourning the loss of the EU's so-called freedom of movement, British academics in particular seem to be mortified by the prospect that they might have to rub shoulders with people from outside Europe in an airport queue when they travel to the continent to attend their international conferences or fly to their holiday homes in France and Italy.

In their 2002 paper on Eutopia, Nicolaïdis and Howse saw Eutopianism as being characterised by the rejection of atavistic nationalism and fascist nihilism. They claimed that the grandness and richness of Europe's political humanism was too great to be confined to the nation-state, necessitating that it overspill national borders.[82] Yet, as has been seen since the outbreak of the crisis in 2008, it is the EU that has pursued its goals with a willful and blithe destructiveness that can only be called nihilistic – in the laying waste of the Greek economy, the generational stagnation of Italy, the mindless blundering into geopolitical rivalry with Russia, consigning so many refugees and migrants to the watery mass grave of the Mediterranean. Nicolaïdis and Howse contrasted the EU favourably with those other grand institutions of global governance, the World Trade Organization, the International Monetary Fund, and the Group of Eight, noting that the EU "has not had its Seattle ... or Gothenburg" referring to the notorious anti-globalisation riots that accompanied global elite conferences in 1999 and 2001. "Even the last referendums in Denmark or Ireland have not had the dramatic quality of the anti-globalization campaign," they noted.[83] From the vantage point of the third decade of our century, the anarchist "black bloc" riots of the 1990s and early 2000s seem like quaint jousts, disputes between different wings of the cosmopolitan elite. Compare this to the grinding weekly brutality of the French riot police battling the *gilets jaunes* protestors continuously over many months. Nor could anyone deny the dramatic quality of the 2015 and 2016 Greek and British referenda. Whereas Carr saw inter-war liberal utopianism extruded back into Europe through the device of American power and money, today the Americans cannot be blamed for the woes of Eutopia; the reckless pursuit of the harmony of interests is ultimately the fault of Europeans themselves.[84]

All the elements that Nicolaïdis and Howse identified as constituting Eutopianism point us to the Carrite conclusion. The economic dirigisme that Howse and Nicolaïdis claimed elevated the EU above the WTO is moot in light of the crushing austerity imposed across the EU since the financial crisis, in light of the contradictions and maladies of the Eurozone, in light of the persistent neoliberal rulings of the ECJ. All the other elements identified by Howse and Nicolaïdis – the fact that Eutopianism incorporates politicians and leading political, legal and constitutional theorists rather than merely anonymous trade functionaries like the WTO, crowned with what they openly celebrate as an explicitly political court in the form of the ECJ – all this only signals how far Eutopianism has become an elite project, with power shielded from public pressure, scrutiny and democratic accountability. Carr declared in 1936 that if "European democracy binds its living body to the putrefying corpse of the 1919 settlement, it will merely be committing a particularly unpleasant form of suicide."[85] Today we can say with equal certainty that if European democracy binds its living body to the putrefying corpse of the 1999 settlement – that is, the Eurozone – it will also be committing a particularly unpleasant form of suicide.

As we saw at the start of this chapter, Fukuyama's bowdlerised *Washington Post*-Hegelianism led him to see the EU as the end of history. For Fukuyama, the post-historic world of the European common market comprised "flabby, prosperous, self-satisfied, inward-looking, weak-willed states whose grandest project was nothing more heroic than the creation of the Common Market."[86] Yet Hegel himself was an Americanist; he thought it was America that would carry the burden of the future: "America is therefore the land of the future, where, in the ages that lie before us, the burden of the world's history shall reveal itself ... It is a land of desire for all those who are weary of the historical lumber-room of old Europe."[87] Two centuries later, Eutopians still sullenly resist the inexorable weight of Hegel's judgement, desperately hoping that their fastidious and intricately crafted regulations on consumer rights and suppression of Internet freedoms can win them an audience in Washington, Brasília, Tokyo, Beijing and Delhi. Those who are most resistant to Europe's decline are of course the decolonial Eutopians who shrilly decry Eurocentrism in the desperate attempt to prolong their own importance in the face of the extra-European world in Asia and the Americas.

Clearing out the lumber room need not be such a wearisome task, and it is in any case sorely belated. There is much to be done to recover from the calamitous Eurozone, to restore, renew and extend democracy, to recover from austerity and forge a new raft of democratised international relationships after having dismantled the supranational EU. Far from consigning Europe to passivity, the dismantling of the EU is the task of a lifetime. Actually making Europe into a "post-historic" paradise need be neither flabby nor weak-willed, as the science fiction author Ken MacLeod indicates in a vision for a post-historic Europe at once more appealing and historically apposite than anything offered by either neo-conservatives or Eutopians:

> ... this is Europe. We took it from nobody; we won it from the bare soil that the ice left. The bones of our ancestors, and the stones of their works, are everywhere. Our liberties were won in wars and revolutions so terrible that we do not fear our governors: they fear us. Our children giggle and eat ice-cream in the palaces of past rulers. We snap our fingers at kings. We laugh at popes. When we have built up tyrants, we have brought them down. And we have nuclear *fucking* weapons.[88]

Having given the world the Enlightenment, Western philosophy, bourgeois revolution, democracy and individual rights, industrial capitalism, *and* the critique of all of these, Europe is surely entitled to at last withdraw from the world-historic stage.

Conclusion: Beyond the Twenty Years' Crisis

One would have to be very old to remember the original twenty years' crisis today. To have at least some meaningful memory of the interbellum, one would have to have been born probably not much later than 1929. My own views of the twenty years' crisis – before I learned to call it that – were shaped by my grandparents, and especially my grandmothers, both of whom were more loquacious (at least with respect to the twenty years' crisis) than my grandfathers, whose memories of the interbellum were perhaps overshadowed by their having been veterans in the conflict that came after it.

For my British grandmother, the interbellum was simply the Depression, and *my* abiding memory of *her* memory of the twenty years' crisis was – on top of hunger – a truncated early education (despite academic success) driven by the need to work, the deep and abiding humiliations of poverty, under-paid piece-work in poor working conditions, as well as the hardship and suffering that came with unemployment and the miserly inter-war welfare system. My Yugoslav grandmother, who was more well-to-do in her childhood, had fonder memories of the 1930s, which for her was the "time of the old Yugoslav kingdom." Sepia-tinted, I have no doubt, as a result of the hardships that she had to endure afterwards. She would have been too young to appreciate the political crisis of the regency that followed the assassination of King Aleksandar I in 1934, as well as being fortunate enough to be sheltered from the rural economic hardship so eloquently described by Vojislav Marinković, the Yugoslav statesman of the interbellum whose speeches in Geneva – at the "Com-mission for European Union" no less – Carr deployed to great effect in criticizing the free trade illusions of the interbellum.[1]

Yet the twenty years' crisis has persisted, right through to the end of the last century. In the aftermath of the invasion of Iraq, my British grandmother wondered whether US president George W. Bush was a new Hitler bent on world domination. I demurred, pointing out that he wasn't that bad and that in any case, the Americans already ruled the world so had no need to conquer it. That left me with the conundrum of trying to explain the crude irrationality of the Iraq invasion. Her observation was a reflection of a life shaped by the twenty years' crisis and its legacy, but also reflected an early-twenty-first-century media that still framed itself around narratives inherited from the interbel-lum. In this case, it was the notion that President Bush's subversion of international law and rampant campaigns of military conquest would lead to greater international tension that would lead in turn to global collapse. Today of course, Donald Trump is cast as the fascist. How can it be that basic questions of international order are still being framed around questions taken from my grandparents' childhood and youth – a continuous morbid cycle of depression, fascism, fraying international law, international collapse and world war?

Perhaps Carr predicted this as well, when he envisaged international politics as necessarily condemned to oscillate between brash utopian-ism and prudent realism, the one always correcting for the other over time. It has become a familiar bromide that everyone reads the first part of Carr's *Twenty Years' Crisis*, where he disparages liberal utopian-ism, but not the latter part where he changes tack and offers his own utopian solutions.[2] This has prompted some to consider what blend of utopianism and realism is appropriate – efforts that inevitably end up proving more ideal than the most ideal utopianism, because "utopian realism," like Goldilocks's porridge, will of course by definition never be either too hot or too cold, but a perfect blend of each. Utopian realism will always be perfect and therefore above critique.

The fault is Carr's own for polarizing the two extremes of utopianism and realism in such a way that he would end up motivating the search for combination and balance of the two extremes in response – and indeed, he began this task himself in the latter part of *The Twenty Years' Crisis* and in his later books, such as *Conditions of Peace*. I propose no such combinations here. As we have seen, one of the problems with the utopianism of our day is that in some ways it is *insufficiently* utopian – actual utopianism of the classical socialist mould would be energising rather than enervating. Moreover, when Carr claimed that the pendulum of international politics was destined to swing forever between utopianism and realism, he probably did not envisage that we would also be trapped in the twenty years' crisis itself forever. I have suggested in this book that the twenty years' crisis of our post-Cold War liberal international order can be usefully studied through the optics provided by E.H. Carr, not only to identify similarities but also differences, and that both exercises are equally instructive. Yet the very fact that we can still usefully apply Carr's analysis in this way also makes clear how little we have progressed beyond it.

In earlier chapters we saw the claim made that there was never a "first great debate" in which Carr was a participant. The result of this, however, is that the discipline of IR has thus never had any great debate at all: pulling out the base does not mean that the next levels simply collapse on top of the absent space where the first level used to be. The "second great debate," inspired by the behaviourist revolution in social science, cannot substitute for the first, and the "third great debate" cannot substitute for the second, and so on. Whether these great debates produced any intellectual progress has been legitimately questioned, but what differentiates the "first great debate" from the others is that it was less internal – it was the only great debate in the history of the discipline in which theoretical development was explicitly linked to political interests and the changing structure of international order. As we have seen, IR theory, and especially Critical IR, has since become unmoored from international politics. Without a founding great debate, the history of the discipline simply becomes an eternal present. I have argued that liberal utopianism has assumed new forms and guises and is highly prominent in international affairs today, not only in terms of liberal internationalist and cosmopolitan politics, but also and especially camouflaged by constructivist and critical theory. Worse, however, the outlooks of our twenty years' crisis carry none of the revolutionary hope and optimism of the original twenty years' crisis, while retaining and indeed exacerbating all its worst aspects: liberal suspicion of mass democracy, dogmatic ideology affirming the status quo, and in Europe, an institutional rigidity as backwards as the gold standard and Versailles settlement, in the form of rampant technocracy and monetary union without a fiscal union.

Thus, if the intellectual archaeologists of the discipline of IR are right when they tell us that the first great debate never happened, the implication seems to be that we are now condemned to repeat it, without resolution, forever. Liberal international order did not die in 1939 and the puncturing of *bien pensant* liberal illusions by realist wiseacres has been a recurring motif of international politics ever since.[3] As Alison McQueen stresses, Carr shows us how liberalism fails, but not necessarily how it ends.[4] Yet, as we have seen, at the same time the liberal utopianism of our era no longer has the excuse of youthful exuberance, brash American naivety and political infantilism that Carr was generously willing to extend to the liberal idealism of the inter-war period. Our liberal utopians of today, particularly those of the Eutopian variety, show no signs of youthful vigour, only the rickety constitution, incipient dementia and senescent fears of the outside world that attend old age – fears of the Russians and the Chinese, fears of fascism, world war, depression, the revival of xenophobic nationalism ... hazy inherited memories only dimly remembered. The very fact that Carr's analysis still has so much traction today is no accident. It reflects not only the intellectual torpor of the discipline and Carr's perspicacity as a thinker and analyst, but also the fact that the twenty years' crisis is evidently *built into the structure of international political order itself.*

After all, how many times have we been warned of the cataclysmic consequences of a foreign policy of appeasement since 1939? How many times have we been warned since 1945 that economic downturns threaten fascism? How many times have we been warned that the failure to extend international cooperation will inevitably reproduce the fate of the former League of Nations, which fell to fascism? How many wars against fascism have been fought since 1945? From the Soviets refighting Nazis in the Berlin uprising of 1953, to crushing Hungarian fascism in 1956 as well as the failed British attempt to crush Egyptian fascism in 1956, through the wars against Serbian fascism in 1995 and again in 1999 ... to the permanent war against Islamofascism across multiple theatres since 2001, or the wars against Iraqi fascism across 1990 to 2010 ... to the constant demands for war against Syrian fascism since 2011 ... to Putin's intervention against Georgian fascism in 2008 and against Ukrainian fascism in 2014 ... to Ukraine fighting against Putinite fascism. Anti-fascism has launched more wars than fascism ever did. Yet how frequently we continue to be mobilised against fascism, from the demands for Internet censorship to combat the supposed spread of fascism online, through to French president Emmanuel Macron's denunciation of the *gilets jaunes* as fascists, to Eutopian denunciation of Brexiter fascism that ricochets in turn against Brexiters' insistence that continental Europeans should show more gratitude to Britain for having liberated them from fascism (and that the EU is a new German empire in any case). Judging by the current state of international debate, one might be tempted to conclude that everyone is a fascist and political change is itself fascism. Such is the intellectual debasement wrought by anti-fascism.

When Ken Booth and his collaborators spoke of an eighty-year crisis, they were more correct than they knew. It is less that the depth of the world's problems are so dire that they parallel those of the interbellum, as much as the fact that it seems we cannot rouse ourselves to confront our own challenges without having to conjure up the spectre of fascism and refight world wars all over again. We remain collectively trapped in the twenty years' crisis, in a loop of collective illusion around collapsing international cooperation and resurgent fascism. Inasmuch as the liberal international order of the last thirty years is drawing to a close as a result of our most recent twenty years' crisis, we know that it was liberals themselves who brought it to a premature end. While convergent economic globalization was always destined to precipitate the end of unipolarity by boosting the position of subaltern states through economic growth and technological diffusion, liberals hastened its end by their policies across the last twenty years – not least in (re)fighting one too many wars against fascism; wars that would lead to imperial over-reach as a direct result of metaphorical over-extension. Thus it was the humanitarian liberals and neo-conservatives boldly fighting fascism from behind their laptop screens that squandered the gains of the post-Cold War order and provoked new geopolitical rivalries. It was Eutopians who stuffed dynamite into the economic core of Europe when they built the Eurozone in 1999 in order, of course, to get over Europe's fascist past. The peace and prosperity that were supposed to be the spontaneous products of the market and civil society were lost through liberal and neoliberal determination to remake the world order.

Karl Marx's observation about history repeating first as tragedy, then as farce might seem apposite were it not for the fact that its garbled repetition has blunted its force and insight. When Marx sneered at the mid-nineteenth-century Napoleonic pretender Louis Napoleon for hiding "his trivial and repulsive lectures behind the iron death mask of Napoleon [the First],"[5] Marx was criticising the impulse to repeat an earlier phase of French politics in changed circumstances. Yet the Napoleonic pretence was at least intended to restore France to Napoleonic glory. The repetition of the twenty years' crisis over and over again across the last eighty years in changed circumstances is to *avoid* glory and heroism; it achieves its effects by aiming to avert disaster, even though the repetition of the twenty years' crisis means that we hover permanently on the brink of disaster.

Invoking Carr, Ken Booth anticipates a "Great Reckoning" in the middle of our century that will result from nuclear proliferation under conditions of multipolarity, population stress and ecological overload.[6] Yet the fear of imminent catastrophe is precisely what prevents us from tackling our contemporary problems. In Iraq and Afghanistan, the catastrophe has already happened and is ongoing. In Italy and Greece, the catastrophe has already happened – and it will take a generation to recover from the folly of Eutopian economics in those countries. Secular Syrian liberals, nationalists, socialists and leftists have already had their Great Reckoning, and they were found wanting, when they proved themselves too weak to prevent a national democratic revolution against Ba'athist dictatorship from collapsing into a dystopian cosmopolitan jihad. Egyptian secularists, liberals and leftists had their Great Reckoning in 2013 when they chose to replay French nineteenth-century politics by inviting the Egyptian army to rescue them from democracy, their Napoleonic pretender coming in the no less trivial and repulsive form of Colonel-General Abdel Fattah el-Sisi. The European ruling elite confronted their Great Reckoning across 2014 and 2015, when they could have offered the peoples of Europe a vision for fiscal and political union. They were found wanting. The Greek left had its Great Reckoning when they called the 2015 referendum and then accepted Eutopian austerity. They, too, were found wanting ... the list of reckonings goes on. Perversely, the delusions of the new liberal uto-pianism allow us to evade these actual reckonings in fear of a deferred Great Reckoning in the future: the structural deflation and austerity of the Eurozone must be left intact to avoid fascism and war. Democracy in Britain must be thwarted and Brexit reversed to avoid fascism ... it goes on.

Our global and transnational institutions – the United Nations system, including the Bretton Woods institutions, the EU, the paradigm of "responsible sovereignty," are, if not explicitly modelled around the twenty years' crisis, then certainly legitimated by it. That is, they are built around warding off the apocalypse of ultra-nationalism, geno-cide, war, etc., legitimating themselves by keeping us perpetually on the brink of catastrophe. The real critique of the interbellum is to get beyond it, to escape the mental prison in which any political change to international order and the status quo is perceived as threatening immediate collapse and ruination. Indeed, the real positive lesson of our twenty years' crisis is that we have escaped a world war, which, as every school child knows, is supposed to be the denouement of all twenty year crises. Small comfort for the citizens of Syria, Afghanistan, Libya and many other places, but still – the fact that we have (at least at the time of writing!) avoided global war despite the best efforts of liberal internationalists, neo-conservatives and human rights crusaders intent on extending permanent war to Damascus, Caracas, Pyongyang, Tehran and beyond as well as a host of conspiratorial fantasists seeking war with Russia, is positive news in and of itself.

As we have seen, the recreation of liberal utopianism signals a post-political era in which politics has been anathematised – captured, constrained and suppressed through constitutional engineering in post-conflict democratizing states, new transnational humanitarian and international criminal law and courts to tame the excesses of sovereign power, vast ethical systems of human rights, new international regula-tory regimes to coordinate states through to economic globalization to resolve questions of need and want by drowning every distributional conflict in a rising tide of prosperity. As we saw, constructivist and critical international theories also confounded themselves in the eva-sion of politics, vesting themselves instead in global social movements, carried forth by a globalization that they would belatedly seek to shape. With the decline of unipolarity and the fragmentation of globalization, the question of political power is becoming harder to avoid.

Stefan Eich and Adam Tooze note that there has been a strengthening counterweight of political realism in response to the rampant liberalism of the post-Cold War era. These new realists range from "disenchanted liberals to Nietzschean feminists, from neo-Machiavellians to left Schmittians," most of whom share a reverence for Max Weber. Doubtless, many of the realist barbs that Weber uses to such great effect in his century-old "Politics as Vocation" lecture would lodge themselves deep in the flesh of contemporary liberal utopianism. Weber's insistence that policy is "the means of power and violence" that involves a "pact with diabolical powers" and his indictment of the idea "that only good can come from good and only evil from evil" is a salutary reminder for our time. This "creed of the political infant" as Weber put it, would indeed be a fitting epitaph for the era of humanitarian warfare and the devastation that has come from its infantile good intentions.[7]

Yet is IR realism sufficient to our needs? As we saw in previous chapters, the revival of classical realism in IR carries with it many of the traits of post-political liberalism, so much so that it might best be called "cosmopolitan realism."[8] Slavoj Žižek has observed that contemporary Western culture is characteristically "decaffeinated" – that is, many domains of life have had the dangerous elements pre-emptively extracted to avoid risk. Thus we have coffee without caffeine, beer with low or zero-alcohol, tightly controlled algorithmic dating in place of falling in love – and in politics, wars with zero casualties (for our side), and we might add in human rights, rights without rights … To this series we might also add that we now have realism without realism – that the intellectual revival of classical realism in IR offers us a decaffeinated version in which the dangerous, disruptive elements – those of political power, the state and political interests – have been extracted, leaving a more tepid brew barely distinguishable from the proverbial liberal idealism, no less focussed on cosmopolitanism, ethics, international cooperation. It is probably already too late to make realism more real again.

In the domestic sphere, so-called left Schmittianism has, unsurprisingly, fed through into the delusions of left Euro-populism, such as Podemos in Spain and Syriza in Greece.[9] Weber's own dramatic posture of crisis offers us only an atavistic revisionism as the basis for politics.

This would not serve us well, as it would merely act to reproduce our problem – to recreate the spectre of catastrophism. Unlike Carr, Weber was, after all, writing at the start of the twenty years' crisis, not at its end, and his political realism evinced his desire to overthrow the nascent Paris peace system. Invoking Weberian realism today would simply reproduce the twenty years' crisis, not help us get beyond it – not to mention the fact that Weber's putative realism is built on a foundation of romantic political existentialism and bitter revanchist nationalism.

Carr, by contrast, was cooler about such things and he preferred to draw on Machiavelli for his political realism rather than the ancient Indian courtier Kauṭilya, whom Weber ostentatiously exalted as a political visionary many centuries in advance of the great Florentine. From Machiavelli, Carr took not the facile injunction to ruthless guile, so much as stressing the process of causation in history – the insight that theory had to be derived from practice rather than vice versa, and that politics is not a function of ethics.[10] What Machiavelli lacked, Carr suggested, was historicism – the notion that overall trends and deep patterns were discernible in historical evolution. It was this last that made Carr's realist thought pragmatic and "realistic" in the sense that it would help mould policy to the grain of historical development rather than around imagined ideals.[11] This led Carr to imagine that the nation-state was vanishing from history, that mass politics would be sublimated into legitimate supranationalism, and that the Soviet continental command economy was the paradigmatic model of the future.

Yet Carr also endorsed Hegel's dictum that "world history is the world court."[12] Given the outcomes of the twentieth century, we can see that – unlike the actually existing world courts in Strasbourg and The Hague – the pitiless court of world history *does* recognise more than money and might.[13] For how else to explain the extinction of the Soviet dinosaur that so overawed Carr in the twentieth century? More recently, the failure of might to make right can be seen in the awesome sight of millions of citizens of Hong Kong taking to the streets of their city to protest the despotic rule of the central government in Beijing in June 2019, in the remarkable persistence of the *gilets jaunes* protestors in France braving the thuggery of the French state, in the ongoing heroism and tragedy of the Arab Spring that finally spread to Algiers and Khartoum in 2019, in the voters of Istanbul facing down the autocratic Turkish president Recep Erdoğan in the mayoral elections of June 2019, and, most terribly and bloodily, in the failure of US empire-building across the Greater Middle East. Thus, to Carr's vision of Machiavellianism, we might add a fourth dimension – that of political realism being a necessary mainstay of freedom, its maintenance requiring a robustly collective vision of the dynamics of political power.[14]

One of Carr's central claims was that the political dynamics of the twentieth century were fundamentally different from those of the nineteenth. Luckily, echoing Carr, we can say that the dynamics of twenty-first-century politics will be fundamentally different from those of the twentieth.[15] Yet acknowledging this also means being willing to relinquish the framework of the twenty years' crisis, too. At the same time, the problems identified by Carr – the breakdown of the nineteenth-century liberal order under the impact of mass political participation and the decline of a competitive market economy[16] – remain our problems too. This is not least because the twentieth century failed to find a lasting resolution to these crises, whether from left or right. Carr's own readiness to vest the USSR with the resolution to these crises is a token of this failure, too. The question for us is, will we be able to succeed where the twentieth century failed?

Notes

PREFACE

1 Lest the intellectual hegemony of the Animal Kingdom in IR be doubted, see Matthew Leep, "Stray Dogs, Post-Humanism and Cosmopolitan Belongingness: Interspecies Hospitality in Times of War," *Millennium* 47, no. 1 (2018): 45–66.

2 In reality, these are mostly routine debates about alternative actors to the nation-state that are grandiloquently scaled up into supposed "different ontologies."

3 The phrase is James Rosenau's, cited in Kalevi J. Holsti, "Retreat from Utopia: International Relations Theory, 1945–70," *Canadian Journal of Political Science/Revue canadienne de science politique* 4, no. 2 (1971): 172.

4 Kevork Oskanian, "Carr Goes East: Reconsidering Power and Inequality in a Post-Liberal Eurasia," *European Politics and Society* 20, no. 2 (2019): 172–89; see also Richard Sakwa, "The Cold

Peace: Russo-Western Relations as a Mimetic Cold War," *Cambridge Review of International Affairs* 26, no. 1 (2013): 203–24.

5 The arguments in that paper appear in Philip Cunliffe, *Cosmopolitan Dystopia: International Intervention and the Failure of the West* (Manchester: Manchester University Press, 2020).

6 See, e.g., Peter Wilson, "The Myth of the 'First Great Debate,'" in *Eighty Years' Crisis: International Relations 1919–1999*, ed. Tim Dunne, Michael Cox, Ken Booth (Cambridge: Cambridge University Press, 1998).

7 Woodrow Wilson, cited in E.H. Carr, *The Twenty Years' Crisis 1919–1939: An Introduction to the Study of International Relations* (Basingstoke: Palgrave, 2001), 8.

8 V.I. Lenin, cited in Carr, *Twenty Years' Crisis*, 97.

9 Carr, cited in Wilson, "Myth," 1.

10 There is a performative contradiction in the structure of this claim, as the impressive array of evidence marshalled against the notion of a "first great debate" in the discipline shows that a debate did indeed happen – it was simply in a form that does not fit the frameworks of contemporary scholarship, taking place as it did in reviews of leading newspapers and in Carr's subsequent war-time books on the shape of the post-war order. It was also a debate that included at different points some of the leading thinkers of the era, such as Alfred Zimmern, Arnold Toynbee, F.A. von Hayek, Martin Wight, Hans J. Morgenthau, among others. In other words, the fact that the first great debate did not take place in learned journals does not mean that a debate did not take place. See also Luke Ashworth, "Did the Realist-Idealist Great Debate Really Happen? A Revisionist History of International Relations," *International Relations* 16, no. 1 (2002): 33–51.

11 Stephen Walt, cited in John J. Mearsheimer, *The Great Delusion: Liberal Dreams and International Realities* (New Haven: Yale University Press, 2018), 130. In his book, Mearsheimer differentiates between what he calls "progressive" liberalism and "modus vivendi" liberalism, but it is a forced division that does not capture the actual evolution of liberal internationalism.

12 I owe this characterisation to Prof Georg Sørenson, who delivered the keynote lecture at an UPTAKE workshop at the University of Kent, on 2 November 2017.

13 Mearsheimer, *Great Delusion*, 10.

14 I owe these points to Milan Babík and Mick Cox. A partial exception to this trend is William Wohlforth.

INTRODUCTION

1 See for instance, Rodney Jefferson and Wojciech Moskwa, "The Ugly Side of Poland's Booming Economy," *Bloomberg* 31 July 2018. https://www.bloomberg.com/news/articles/2018-07-31/the-ugly-side-of-

poland-s-booming-economy (accessed 21 February 2019). On Viktor Orbán's resistance to international financial institutions in Hungary, see Juliet Johnson and Andrew Barnes, "Financial nationalism and its international enablers: The Hungarian Experience," *Review of International Political Economy* 22, no. 3 (2015): 535–69.

2 These last points were raised by Mick Cox at a roundtable, "Carr's Crisis and Ours: 1939/2019," British International Studies Association annual conference, London, 12–14 June 2019.

3 On Carr's approach, see Seán Molloy, *The Hidden History of Realism: A Geneaology of Power Politics* (Basingstoke: Palgrave, 2006), 55.

4 There are various ways to differentiate the strands of critical theorizing in IR. Some use the capitalized "Critical Theory" to refer to those IR theorists who have sought to deploy the ideas of the Frankfurt School, and lower-case "critical theory" to refer to a wider field of post-structuralism, feminism, post-humanism, and so on. Nicholas Michelson differentiates between "synoptic" and "anti-synoptic" theory, the former including thinkers such as Robert Cox, Andrew Linklater, Barry Buzan and Mark Neufeld, the latter including Richard K. Ashley, David Campbell R.B.J. Walker. Nicholas Michelsen, "A Critique of Critical International Relations: What is a Minor International Theory?" Draft. I will simply refer to "critical theory" throughout this volume to mean both these strands.

5 E.H. Carr, *The Twenty Years' Crisis 1919–1939: An Introduction to the Study of International Relations* (Basingstoke: Palgrave, 2001), 80.

6 This section draws on the superb summary in Graham Evans, "E.H. Carr and International Relations," *Review of International Studies* 1, no. 2 (1975): 79–81, and to a lesser extent on Hans J. Morgenthau's "The Political Science of E.H. Carr," Review of E.H. Carr's *The Twenty Years' Crisis*, "Conditions of Peace, Nationalism and After, The Soviet Impact on the Western World," *World Politics* 1, no. 1 (1948): 127–34.

7 Carr, *Twenty Years' Crisis*, 4.

8 Ibid., 6.

9 Ibid., cv.

10 Ibid., 97.

11 Ibid., 50.

12 Ibid., 45.

13 See, e.g., Nancy Fraser, "The End of Progressive Neoliberalism," *Dissent*, 2 January 2017, www.dissentmagazine.org/online_articles/progressive-neoliberalism-reactionary-populism-nancy-fraser (accessed 30 May 2019).

14 Carr, *Twenty Years' Crisis*, 38.

15 Progressive neoliberals and critical scholars shared in this assumption inasmuch as they cast themselves against the Eurocentric, materialistic, classist, and essentialist assumptions of Marxism.

16 Carr, *Twenty Years' Crisis*, 71.

17   Ibid.

18   Ibid., 80.

19   Slavoj Žižek, *Like a Thief in Broad Daylight: Power in the Era of Post Humanity* (London: Penguin, 2018), 211.

20   John Lewis Gaddis, *We Now Know: Rethinking Cold War History* (Oxford: Clarendon Press, 1998), 234.

21   See Michael Cox, "E.H. Carr and the Crisis of Twentieth-Century Liberalism," *Millennium: Journal of International Studies* 38, no. 3 (2010): 532 and passim.

22   See further Sean Iling, "Richard Rorty's Prescient Warnings for the American Left," *Vox*, 2 February 2019, https://www.vox.com/policy-and-politics/2017/2/9/14543938/donald-trump-richard-rorty-election-liberalism-conservatives (accessed 25 June 2019).

23   See also Toby Dodge, *Iraq: From War to a New Authoritarianism* (London: International Institute for Strategic Studies, 2013), passim.

24   Arguably the most perspicacious analyst here was from outside IR – namely, the demographer Emmanuel Todd in his 2003 book *After the Empire: The Breakdown of the American Order*, trans. C. John Delogu, Introduction by Michael Lind (New York: Columbia University Press, 2003).

25   See, e.g., Branko Milanović, "Kate Raworth's Economics of Miracles," http://glineq.blogspot.com/2018/06/kate-raworths-economics-of-miracles.html (accessed 8 March 2019).

26   Samuel Huntington is the classic exemplar here. See, e.g., Huntington, *Political Order in Changing Societies*, foreword by Francis Fukuyama (New Haven: Yale University Press, 2006).

27   Sandra Whitworth, *Men, Militarism, and UN Peacekeeping: A Gendered Analysis* (Boulder, CO: Lynne Rienner Publishers, 2004), 186.

28   David Campbell, "Why Fight: Humanitarianism, Principles, and Post-structuralism," *Millennium: Journal of International Studies* 27, no. 3 (1998): 497–521.

29   See, e.g., contributions in Albrecht Schnabel and Ramesh Thakur, *Kosovo and the Challenge of Humanitarian Intervention: Selective Indignation, Collective Action and International Citizenship* (Tokyo: United Nations University Press, 2000); and Nicholas J. Wheeler and Tim Dunne, "Good International Citizenship: A Third Way for British Foreign Policy," *International Affairs* 74, no. 4 (1998): 847–70.

30   See David Campbell, *National Deconstruction: Violence, Identity and Justice in Bosnia* (Minneapolis: University of Minnesota Press, 1998).

31   Campbell, *National Deconstruction*, 223–4.

32   On just war and a wider critique of the cosmopolitan order, see Danilo Zolo, *Cosmopolis: Prospects for World Government* (Cambridge: Polity, 1997).

33   James Rubin, "Base Motives," *Guardian*, 8 May 2004, www.theguardian.com/books/2004/may/08/highereducation.usa (accessed 8 March 2019).

34 Michael Hardt and Antonio Negri, *Empire* (Cambridge, MA: Harvard University Press).

35 Robert W. Cox, "Social Forces, States and World Orders: Beyond International Relations Theory," *Millennium* 10, no. 2 (1981): 147.

36 See inter alia Daniel H. Nexon and Iver B. Neumann, *Harry Potter and International Relations* (Oxford: Rowman and Littlefield, 2006); On "Hello Kitty," see the programme of a 2015 workshop on the matter, https://www.scribd.com/document/264498177/Hello-Kitty-and-International-Relations (accessed 19 November 2019).

37 See inter alia Robert A. Saunders and Jack Holland, "The Ritual of Beer Consumption as Discursive Intervention: Effigy, Sensory Politics, and Resistance in Contemporary IR," *Millennium: Journal of International Studies* 46, no. 2 (2018): 119–41; Rune S. Anderson, Juha A. Viori, and Xavier Guillaume, "Chromatology of Security: Introducing Colours to Visual Security Studies," *Security Dialogue* 46, no. 5 (2015): 440–57.

38 Ken Booth, "Security in Anarchy: Utopian Realism in Theory and Practice," *International Affairs* 67, no. 3 (1991), 544.

39 Robert A. Saunders and Rhys Crilley, "Pissing on the Past: The Highland Clearances, Effigial Resistance, and the Everyday Politics of the Urinal," *Millennium* (2019): 3.

40 Ibid., 22.

41 In a remarkable instance of life imitating art, IR was subject to a hoax in 2014 that turned out to be predictive of the discipline's development: a bogus call for papers to consider "acoustics" in international relations was circulated, and can still be found here: https://groups.google.com/forum/#!topic/isa-ips/KhkfyWYHpG4 (accessed 21 June 2019).

42 Michelsen, "A Critique of Critical International Relations," 5.

43 One such panel was "No Match for a Good Blaster at Your Side: Star Wars and International Security" The video below was used to help advertise the above panel which its participants described as a "teaser trailer," https://www.youtube.com/watch?v=eQUBzKdpZ5Y (accessed 9 June 2019). Another example is "Game of Thrones: Empirical Investigations," which took place during the ISA's 2015 annual conference. The "teaser trailer" for this can be found here: https://www.youtube.com/watch?v=bYYXiW7lYcA (accessed 9 June 2019).

44 In retrospect there were other key turnings points in 2016 too, in Turkey and Syria – and these will be examined more in the next chapter.

45 For a compelling counter-argument against the notion of emergent multipolarity, cf. Øystein Tunsjø, *The Return of Bipolarity in World Politics: China, the United States and Geostructural Realism* (New York: Columbia University Press, 2018).

46 Tim Dunne, Lene Hansen, and Colin Wight, "The End of International Relations Theory?" *European Journal of International Relations* 19, no. 3 (2013): 412–13.

47 David A. Lake, "Theory is Dead, Long Live Theory: The End of the Great Debates and the Rise of Eclecticism in International Relations," *European Journal of International Relations* 19, no. 3 (2013): 567–87.

48 Cameron Harrington, "The Ends of the World: International Relations and the Anthropocene," *Millennium: Journal of International Studies* 44, no. 3 (2016): 481.

49 Anthony Burke, Stefanie Fishel, Audra Mitchell, Simon Dalby, Daniel J. Levine, "Planet Politics: A Manifesto from the End of IR," *Millennium: Journal of International Studies* 44, no. 3 (2016): 4.

50 Harrington, "Ends of the World," 491.

51 Matt McDonald and Audra Mitchell, "Introduction" in *Reflections on the Post Human in International Relations: The Anthropocene, Security and Ecology*, ed. Clara Eroukhmanoff and Matt Harker (E-International Relations, 2017), 5.

52 See, in general, Catarina Kinnvall, "Gayatri Chakravorty Spivak," in *Critical Theorists and International Relations*, ed. Jenny Edkins and Nick Vaughan-Williams (Abingdon: Routledge, 2009), 320–1.

53 This point is inspired by James Heartfield, *The "Death of the Subject" Explained* (Sheffield: Sheffield Hallam University Press, 2002), passim and ch. 7.

54 Burke et al., "Planet Politics," 17–18.

55 Carr, *Twenty Years' Crisis*, 78.

56 Burke et al., "Planet Politics," 3.

57 Harrington, "Ends of the World," 480.

58 Jairus Victor Grove, *Savage Ecology: War and Geopolitics at the End of the World* (Durham: Duke University Press, 2019), 25.

59 Ibid., 45. On Colin Powell, see William Safire, "If you break it ...," *New York Times*, 17 October 2004.

60 Ibid., 27.

61 On the geopolitics of global warming in the Arctic for instance, see Nastassia Astrasheuskaya and Henry Foy, "Polar Powers: Russia's Bid for Supremacy in the Arctic Ocean," *Financial Times*, 28 April 2019.

62 Carr, *Twenty Years' Crisis,* 80.

63 Cynthia Weber, "Why Is There No Queer International Theory?," *European Journal of International Relations* 21, no. 1 (2015): 16.

64 Further to the pervasive influence of excessive theorising in British IR, see Chris Brown, "IR Theory in Britain – The New Black?" *Review of International Studies* 32, no. 4 (2006): 677–87.

65 See John J. Mearsheimer, "E.H. Carr vs. Idealism: The Battle Rages On," *International Relations* 19, no. 2 (2005): 139–52.

66 Carr, cited in Jonathan Haslam, *The Vices of Integrity: E.H. Carr 1892–1982* (London: Verso, 1999), 252.

67 Carr, cited in Babík, "Realism as Critical Theory," 511.

68 For an example of the conflation of (supposed) academic marginalization with actual political marginalization and social exclusion, see Richard K. Ashley and R.B.J. Walker, "Introduction: Speaking the Language of Exile: Dissident Thought in International Studies," *International Studies Quarterly* 34, no. 3 (1990): 263 and passim.

69 Paul Cammack, "RIP IPE," *Papers in the Politics of Global Competitiveness*, no. 7, Institute for Global Studies, Manchester Metropolitan University (2007): 17 and passim.

70 The classic statement of this view is Richard K. Ashley, "Untying the Sovereign State: A Double Reading of the Anarchy *problematique*," *Millennium* 17, no. 2 (1988): 227–62.

71 Ibid., 29.

72 Carr, *Twenty Years' Crisis,* 87.

73 Mearsheimer, "The Battle Rages On." In Carr's day, what is today Aberystwyth University was the University College of Aberystwyth.

74 On the counter-hegemonic status of Carr's work, see Tim Dunne, "Theories as Weapons: E.H. Carr and International Relations," in *E.H. Carr: A Critical Appraisal*, ed. Michael Cox (Basingstoke: Palgrave, 2000).

75 For a useful overview of "Carr Studies," see Babík, "Realism as Critical Theory," 498–9.

76 Keith Smith, "The Realism That Did Not Speak Its Name: E.H. Carr's Diplomatic Histories of the Twenty Years' Crisis," *Review of International Studies* 43, no. 3 (2017): 493.

77 On Carr's "ethics," see Haro L. Karkur, "Debating Global Justice with Carr: The Crisis of Laissez Faire and the Legitimacy Problem in the Twenty-first Century," *Journal of International Political Theory* (2019).

CHAPTER ONE

1 These events are covered in E.H. Carr, *International Relations between the Two World Wars 1919–1939* (London: Macmillan, 1947).

2 G.J. Ikenberry, "The End of Liberal International Order?," *International Affairs* 94, no. 1 (2018): 7–23; Beate Jahn, "Liberal Internationalism: Historical Trajectory and Current Prospects," *International Affairs* 94, no. 1 (2018): 43–61.

3 George H.W. Bush, "George Bush's Speech to the UN General Assembly," *Guardian*, 12 September 2002, www.theguardian.com/world/2002/sep/12/iraq.usa3 (accessed 8 March 2019).

4 For an alternative account of the institutional development of the discipline, see Brian C. Schmidt, *The Political Discourse of Anarchy, A Disciplinary History of International Relations* (Albany, NY: SUNY Press 1998).

5 For a revisionist account of Woodrow Wilson, see also Adam Tooze, *The Deluge: The Great War and the Remaking of Global Order 1916–1931* (London: Penguin, 2016).

6 On the various versions of liberal internationalism, see, e.g., G.J. Iken-berry, "Liberal Internationalism 3.0: America and the Dilemmas of Liberal World Order," *Perspectives on Politics* 7, no. 1 (2009): 71–87.

7 See also Domenico Losurdo, *Liberalism: A Counter-History* (London: Verso, 2014), 7–9.

8 See also Inis L. Claude, Jr., "The Growth of International Institutions," in *The Aberystwyth Papers: International Politics 1919–1969,* ed. Brian Porter (Oxford: Oxford University Press, 1972). See also Carr's account of the nineteenth century in his *Nationalism and After* (London: Macmillan, 1945).

9 For an account of how Carr's wider work relates to IR, see Keith Smith, "The Realism That Did Not Speak Its Name: E.H. Carr's Diplomatic Hist-ories of the Twenty Years' Crisis," *Review of International Studies* 43, no. 3 (2017): 475–93, and, more widely, Seán Molloy, *The Hidden History of Real-ism: A Genealogy of Power Politics* (Basingstoke: Palgrave, 2006), passim.

10 Against the spurious charge that Carr's analysis was "Eurocentric," see Haro L. Karkour, "Debating Global Justice with Carr: The Crisis of Laissez Faire and the Legitimacy Problem in the Twenty-First Century," *Journal of International Political Theory* (2019): fns. 8, 14.

11 Carr, *The Twenty Years' Crisis 1919–1939: An Introduction to the Study of Inter-national Relations* (Basingstoke: Palgrave, 2001), Introduction by Michael Cox, 58.

12 Ibid.

13 Ibid., fns. 37, 61; see also Carr, *Conditions of Peace* (London: Macmillan, 1942), 106.

14 Ibid., 68.

15 Ibid., 101.

16 Ibid., 109.

17 Ibid., 117.

18 Ibid., 212.

19 Ibid., 117.

20 Ibid., 214.

21 Carr, cited in Jonathan Haslam, *The Vices of Integrity: E.H. Carr 1892–1982* (London: Verso, 1999), 85.

22 Ibid., 153.

23 Carr, cited in Stefan Collini, "Historian of the Future," *Times Literary Sup-plement,* 7 March 2008, 15.

24 Ibid., 29.

25 Carr, *Twenty Years' Crisis,* 58–9.

26 Chris Giles, "Ethiopia is Now Africa's Fastest Growing Economy," CNN, 24 April 2018, www.edition.cnn.com/2018/04/24/africa/africa-largest-economy/index.html (accessed 20 February 2019).

27 "The excellence of the British civil service," claimed Carr, "is partly due to the ease with which the bureaucratic mentality accommodates itself to the

empirical tradition of British politics." As a former foreign office mandarin himself, doubtless Carr would find much to query in the conduct of Brexit negotiations. Carr, *Twenty Years' Crisis*, 16.

28   Ibid., 218.

29   Carr, *Nationalism and After* (London: Macmillan, 1945), 30.

30   Here I only discuss Carrian notions of crisis. For further consideration on conceptualising crisis and alternative understandings of crisis, see Rune Møller Stahl, "Ruling the Interregnum: Politics and Ideology in Non-hegemonic Times," *Politics & Society* (2019): doi:0032329219851896. The Elizabeth Wiskemann point I owe to Lucian Ashworth.

31   Tim Dunne, Michael Cox, and Ken Booth, *The Eighty Years' Crisis: International Relations 1919–1999* (Cambridge: Cambridge University Press, 1998), xiv.

32   Michael Cox, "E.H. Carr and the Crisis of Twentieth-Century Liberalism," *Millennium: Journal of International Studies* 38, no. 3 (2010): 523–33.

33   István Hont, "The Permanent Crisis of a Divided Mankind: 'Contemporary Crisis of the Nation State' in Historical Perspective," *Political Studies* 42, no. 1 (1994): 166–231.

34   "'Not Since the Arab Spring Have We Seen So Many Simultaneous Protests' – Why the World is Taking to the Streets," *Economist*, 6 November 2019, https://www.economist.com/podcasts/2019/11/06/not-since-the-arab-spring-have-we-seen-so-many-simultaneous-protests-why-the-world-is-taking-to-the-streets (accessed 11 November 2019). On Iran, see Terry Glavin, "The Uprising in Iran: 'These People Have Nothing to Lose, They're Fearless Now,'" *Maclean's*, 18 November 2019, https://www.macleans.ca/news/world/the-uprising-in-iran-these-people-have-nothing-to-lose-theyre-fearless-now/?fbclid=IwAR1s-VD6p5vqCW-CcipijT5MJW1iaPuWBO5uFt759jBfZqJUsJSirT_W9mM (accessed 19 November 2019). On protests in the Czech Republic in late 2019, see Peter Laca, "Czechs Say Billionaire Leader Must Resign in Mass Protests," *Bloomberg*, 16 November 2019, https://www.bloomberg.com/news/articles/2019-11-16/czechs-demand-resignation-of-billionaire-leader-as-protests-rage?fbclid=IwAR2jOInpzow5vro-pMZAzdqRej8sUzvaVy2K_A8sW-ozntK3Fl_Q8qPwOeY (accessed 19 November 2019).

35   See, in general, Stephen M. Walt, *The Hell of Good Intentions: America's Foreign Policy Elite and the Decline of U.S. Primacy* (New York: Farrar, Straus and Giroux, 2018), 62.

36   See further, Joshua R. Shifrinson Itzkowitz, "Deal or No Deal? The End of the Cold War and the US Offer to Limit NATO Expansion," *International Security* 40, no. 4 (2016): 7–44; Richard Sakwa, *Frontline Ukraine: Crisis in the Borderlands* (London: IB Tauris, 2014).

37   Kevork K. Oskanian, "Carr Goes East: Reconsidering Power and Inequality in a Post-Liberal Eurasia," *European Politics and Society* (2018): 9.

38   Ibid.

39 See further, Michael Cox, "Introduction," to Carr, *Twenty Years' Crisis*, xxvii.

40 Blair, cited in Cameron Abadi, "The Small War That Wasn't," *Foreign Policy*, 2 January 2019, foreignpolicy.com/2019/01/02/the-small-war-that-wasnt/ (accessed 10 March 2019).

41 This is Brian Porter's argument. See also Brian Porter, "E.H. Carr – The Aberystwyth Years, 1936–47," in *E.H. Carr: A Critical Appraisal*, ed. Michael Cox (Basingstoke: Palgrave, 2004), 61.

42 See, e.g., Albrecht Schnabel and Ramesh Thakur, *Kosovo and the Challenge of Humanitarian Intervention: Selective Indignation, Collective Action and International Citizenship* (Tokyo: United Nations University Press, 2000).

43 See also Philip Cunliffe, *Cosmopolitan Dystopia: International Intervention and the Failure of the West* (Manchester: Manchester University Press, 2020).

44 Simon Chesterman, *You, the People: The United Nations, Transitional Administration, and State-Building* (Oxford: Oxford University Press, 2005).

45 It is worth noting that war had already been normalised by the "air occupation" of Iraq following the end of the 1990–91 Gulf War, with a UN-mandated no fly zone curbing Iraqi sovereignty of its airspace. See Andrew Bacevich, *America's War for the Greater Middle East: A Military History* (New York: Random House, 2016), 142–3.

46 Carr, *Twenty Years' Crisis*, 212.

47 Ibid., 198.

48 Ibid., 42.

49 Ibid., 212; see also Carr, *Conditions of Peace*, 222–3.

50 Carr, *Conditions of Peace*, 249.

51 Carr called this process the "socialisation of the nation" in his book *Nationalism and After* (London: Macmillan, 1945). See also Carr, *Conditions of Peace*, 21.

52 Carr, *Twenty Years' Crisis*, 118.

53 This is one of the core arguments of Philip Cunliffe, *Cosmopolitan Dystopia*.

54 This point should be qualified by the discussion that follows, below.

55 Carr, *Twenty Years' Crisis*, 57.

56 Ibid., 126.

57 I owe this point to James Heartfield.

58 See the conclusion in David Chandler, *From Kosovo to Kabul: Human Rights and International Intervention* (London: Pluto Press, 2002).

59 Der Spiegel Staff, "Is Germany's Special Relationship with Russia Ending," *Der Spiegel*, 9 May 2018, www.spiegel.de/international/germany/germany-divided-about-approach-to-russia-a-1206338.html (accessed 10 March 2019).

60 *Economist*, "The Economist at 175: Reinventing Liberalism for the 21st Century," *Economist*, 13 September 2018, www.economist.com/essay/2018/09/13/the-economist-at-175 (accessed 10 March 2018).

61 I owe this insight to Mick Cox.

62 See Philip Cunliffe, *Legions of Peace: UN Peacekeepers from the Global South* (London: C.H. Hurst & Co., 2013).

63 Carr, *Twenty Years' Crisis*, 212.

64 Ibid., 219.

65 See further Claire Ainley, *The New Working Class: How to Win Hearts, Minds and Votes* (Bristol: Policy Press, 2018).

CHAPTER TWO

1 See also Nicholas Michelsen, "A Critique of Critical International Relations: What is a Minor International Theory?," Draft, 20.

2 This is the gravamen of David Chandler's critique in his book *Constructing Global Civil Society: Morality and Power in International Relations* (Basingstoke: Palgrave, 2004), 47.

3 See John J. Mearsheimer, "E.H. Carr vs. Idealism: The Battle Rages On," *International Relations* 19, no. 2 (2005): 139–52; and Beate Jahn, "One Step Forward, Two Steps Back: Critical Theory as the Latest Edition of Liberal Idealism," *Millennium* 27, no. 3 (1998): 613–41. Jahn also makes the case that those she calls the "critical critics" are supporters of international hierarchy.

4 See Jahn, "One Step Forward," esp. 614 for an overview of these earlier critiques.

5 Ibid., fns. 16, 617.

6 Alexander Wendt, "Why a World State is Inevitable," *European Journal of International Relations* 9, no. 4 (2003): 491–542.

7 This section draws heavily on the ideas and argument in James Heartfield, "Marxism and Social Construction," in *Marxism, Mysticism and Modern Theory*, ed. Suke Wolton (Basingstoke: Macmillan, 1996).

8 See, e.g., Nicholas Greenwood Onuf, *World of Our Making: Rules and Rule in Social Theory and International Relations* (Abingdon: Routledge, 2012) and Alexander Wendt, *Social Theory of International Politics* (Cambridge: Cambridge University Press, 1999).

9 See also Suke Wolton, *Lord Hailey, the Colonial Office and Politics of Race and Empire in the Second World War: The Loss of White Prestige* (Basingstoke: Palgrave, 2000).

10 Alexander Wendt, "Anarchy Is What States Make of It: The Social Construction of Power Politics," *International Organization* 46, no. 2 (1992): 391–425.

11 Karl Wolfgang Deutsch, *Political Community and the North American Area* (Princeton: Princeton University Press, 1957).

12 Kenneth N. Waltz, *Theory of International Politics* (Long Grove: Waveland Press, 1979).

13 The classic statement of this model is arguably Martha Finnemore and Kathryn Sikkink, "International Norm Dynamics and Political Change," *International Organization* 52, no. 4 (1998): 887–917.

14 See chapter 6 in Wendt, *Social Theory of International Politics*.

15 Richard Ned Lebow, *The Tragic Vision of Politics: Ethics, Interests and Orders* (Cambridge: Cambridge University Press, 2003), 339.

16 Wendt, "Anarchy Is What States Make of It," 422–4.

17 Ibid., 415–18.

18 Carr, *Twenty Years' Crisis*, 6–7.

19 Emanuel Adler, *Communitarian International Relations: The Epistemic Foundations of International Relations* (Routledge, 2005), 92. I owe this example to Daniel Matthews-Ferrero.

20 The best exemplars of this approach remain Hedley Bull's essays, namely Hedley Bull, "Society and Anarchy in International Relations" and "The Grotian Conception of International Society," in *Diplomatic Investigations: Essays in the Theory of International Politics*, ed. Herbert Butterfield and Martin Wight (London: George Allen and Unwin, 1966).

21 James Heartfield, "Western Imperialism in Denial," Review Essay, *Journal of Intervention and Statebuilding* 3, no. 2 (2009): 296–300.

22 Lebow, *Tragic Vision*, 343–4. Lebow is not a Wendtian constructivist but rather a self-professed classical realist. Nonetheless, he takes IR classical realism as a prototype of constructivism, and is sympathetic to many elements of constructivism – indeed, he criticises Wendt for limiting the purview of his constructivist effects to the systemic, interstate level, thereby overlooking these effects at the state level. For these reasons, this quote from Lebow can be used to illustrate the point here.

23 Richard K. Ashley, "Untying the Sovereign State: A Double Reading of the Anarchy Problematique," *Millennium* 17, no. 2 (1988): 249–50.

24 Rove, quoted in Ron Suskind, "Faith, Certainty and the Presidency of George W. Bush," *NYTimes Magazine*, 17 October 2004.

25 Carr, *Twenty Years' Crisis*, 62.

26 Robert W. Cox, "Social Forces, States and World Orders: Beyond International Relations Theory," *Millennium: Journal of International Studies* 10, no. 2 (1981): 126–55.

27 Ibid., 170.

28 A point made by Jahn, "One Step Forward, Two Steps Back," 638.

29 See also Paul Cammack, "RIP IPE," *Papers in the Politics of Global Competitiveness*, no. 7, Institute for Global Studies, Manchester Metropolitan University (2007). Cammack makes the case that the problem-solvers tended to be more open-minded and reflective than their critical opponents.

30 Ibid.

31 Kenneth N. Waltz, "Reflections on *Theory of International Politics*: A Response to My Critics," in *Neorealism and Its Critics*, ed. Robert O. Keohane (New York: Columbia University Press, 1986), 339.

32 See, for instance, John S. Moolakkattu, "Robert W. Cox and Critical Theory of International Relations," *International Studies* 46, no. 4 (2009): 445.

33 See also Thomas McCarthy, *The Critical Theory of Jürgen Habermas* (Boston:
MIT Press, 1978), 107–8.

34 International solidarity activism with the Palestinians follows a similar
dynamic even though Israel is not a classic Third World state and the
Palestinians were one of the exponents of Third World anti-imperialist
nationalism.

35 Giorgio Shani, "Toward a Post-Western IR: The Umma, Khalsa Panth, and
Critical International Relations Theory," *International Studies Review* 10, no.
4 (2008): 722–34; S.J. Dehghani Firouz, "Emancipating Foreign Policy:
Critical Theory and Islamic Republic of Iran's Foreign Policy," *The Iranian
Journal of International Affairs* 20, no. 3 (2008): 1–26.

36 For a useful short summary of Gramsci's reception in IR as mediated
through Cox, take a look at Mark Rupert, "Gramsci," in *Critical Theorists
and International Relations*, ed. Jenny Edkins and Nick Vaughan-Williams
(New York: Routledge, 2009).

37 Cox, "Social Forces," 130.

38 Gramsci, cited in Robert W. Cox, "Gramsci, Hegemony and International
Relations: An Essay in Method," *Millennium: Journal of International Studies*
12, no. 2 (1983): 165.

39 Ibid., 163.

40 On the fate of Italian Communism, see James Heartfield, "With Enemies
Like These, Who Needs Friends?," *Spiked Online*, 27 January 2012,
https://www.spiked-online.com/2012/01/27/with-enemies-like-these-who-
needs-friends/ (accessed 20 June 2019).

41 Ibid., 442–3.

42 On the Gramscians' turn to (global) civil society, see Moolakkattu, "Robert
W. Cox and Critical Theory of International Relations," 441.

43 See further Lewis Bassett, "From Movementism to Labourism," *Open Democracy*, 28 November 2016, www.opendemocracy.net/uk/lewis-bassett/
from-movementism-to-labourism (accessed 10 March 2019).

44 Jonathan D. Ostry, Prakash Loungani, and Davide Furceri, "Neoliberalism: Oversold?" *Finance & Development* 53, no. 2 (2016), www.imf.org/
external/pubs/ft/fandd/2016/06/ostry.htm (accessed 9 March 2019).

45 Mark Fisher, *Capitalist Realism: Is there no alternative* (London: Zero Books,
2009), 14.

46 Michael Hardt, "Porto Alegre: Today's Bandung?," *New Left Review*, 14
March–April 2002.

47 On this, see further Christoph Harig, "Re-Importing the 'Robust Turn' in
UN Peacekeeping: Internal Public Security Missions of Brazil's Military,"
International Peacekeeping 26, no. 2 (2019): 137–64.

48 Noam Chomsky, "I Just Visited Lula, the World's Most Prominent Political Prisoner. A 'Soft Coup' in Brazil's Election Will Have Global Con-

sequences," *The Intercept*, 2 October 2018. Lula was released on appeal in late 2019. https://theintercept.com/2018/10/02/lula-brazil-election-noam-chomsky/ (accessed 10 March 2019).

49 See Alex Hochuli, "Bolsonaro Rising," *The Baffler*, 29 October 2018, thebaffler.com/latest/bolsonaro-rising-hochuli (accessed 10 March 2019).

50 Cox, "Gramsci," 150.

51 Ibid.

52 Ibid., 151.

53 Ibid., 150.

54 Ibid., 174.

55 Cox, "Social Forces," 135.

56 For a range of these responses, see "Tributes to Robert W. Cox," 29 October 2018, http://ppesydney.net/tributes-to-robert-w-cox/ (accessed 8 June 2019).

57 See the contribution by Heikki Potomäki, ibid.

58 See further Cammack, "RIP IPE," 3; Milan Babík, "Realism as Critical Theory," 496.

59 Potomäki, "Tributes to Robert W. Cox," 29 October 2018.

60 On Cox's hopes for the counter-globalization movement, see Moolakkattu, "Robert W. Cox and Critical Theory of International Relations," 451.

61 Cox, "Social Forces," 128.

62 Kenneth N. Waltz, *Realism and International Politics* (Abingdon: Routledge, 2008), 189.

CHAPTER THREE

1 Emmanuel Macron, "Dear Europe: Brexit is a Lesson for All of Us: It's Time for Renewal," *Guardian*, 4 March 2009, www.theguardian.com/commentisfree/2019/mar/04/europe-brexit-uk (accessed 8 March 2019).

2 Matt Goodwin, Twitter post, 8 April 2019, 7:40 a.m., https://twitter.com/GoodwinMJ/status/1115263043590602752 (accessed 8 June 2019).

3 For an overview of European integration theories related to Carr's work, see Daniel Kenealy and Konstantinos Kostagiannis, "Realist Visions of European Union: E.H. Carr and Integration," *Millennium* 41, no. 2 (2013): 221–46. The argument in this chapter is in pointed contrast to Kenealy and Kostagiannis's line of argument in their paper.

4 Louis Menand, "Francis Fukuyama Postpones the End of History," *New Yorker*, 3 September 2018, www.newyorker.com/magazine/2018/09/03/francis-fukuyama-postpones-the-end-of-history (accessed 7 March 2019).

5 Kalypso Nicolaïdis and Robert Howse, "This is my EUtopia ...: Narrative as Power," *Journal of Common Market Studies* 40, no. 4 (2002): 789.

6 See, e.g., Gurminder K. Bhambra, "Brexit, Trump and Methodological Whiteness: On the Misrecognition of Race and Class," *British Journal of*

Sociology 68, S1 (2017): 214–32. See also Nadine El-Enany, "The Next British Empire," *Progressive Review* 25, no. 1 (2018): 30–8.

7 John M. Hobson, *The Eurocentric Conception of World Politics: Western International Theory 1760–2010* (Cambridge: Cambridge University Press, 2012).

8 For a general critique of the Eurozone, see Costas Lapavitsas, *The Left Case Against the EU* (Cambridge: Polity Press, 2019). Cf. Kenealy and Kostagiannis, "Realist Visions."

9 On Carr's dismissal of those we now know as the "neoliberal economists," see E.H. Carr, *The Soviet Impact on the Western World* (New York: Macmillan, 1947), 45. On neoliberal designs for post-war Europe, see Quinn Slobodian, *Globalists: The End of Empire and the Birth of Neoliberalism* (Cambridge, MA: Harvard University Press, 2018), 112 and passim.

10 Slobodian, *Globalists*, 144 and passim.

11 See Lapavitsas, *Left Case Against the EU*.

12 For all the dystopian scenarios of economic collapse invoked over Brexit, the British economy grew faster than those of Germany, France, and the Eurozone as a whole in the three years since the Brexit referendum in 2016. See Ambrose Evan-Pritchard, "Anti-Brexit lies about Growth Must Be Exposed," *Daily Telegraph*, 12 November 2019.

13 Martin Wolf, "Intolerable Choices for the Eurozone," *Financial Times*, 31 May 2011.

14 See E.H. Carr, *International Relations between the Two World Wars 1919–1939* (London: Macmillan, 1947), esp. ch. 7.

15 Carr, *The Twenty Years' Crisis 1919–1939: An Introduction to the Study of International Relations* (Basingstoke: Palgrave, 2001). Introduction by Michael Cox, 31.

16 Lucio Baccaro, "Tying Your Hands and Getting Stuck: The Italian Political Economy Since the 1970s." Paper presented at "Europe After Brexit" conference, School of Oriental and African Studies, London, September 2018. Draft.

17 See Adam Tooze on these points: *Crashed: How a Decade of Financial Crisis Changed the World* (New York: Penguin, 2018), esp. Part III.

18 See, e.g., Ashoka Mody, *EuroTragedy: A Drama in Nine Acts* (Oxford: Oxford University Press, 2018); Lapavitsas, *Left Case*.

19 This is the substance of Lapavitsas' critique, *Left Case*.

20 Adam Tooze, "The German Impasse," *Social Europe*, 12 November 2019, https://www.socialeurope.eu/the-german-impasse?fbclid=IwAR1P9xuy aOKMnTK5ddlXrVUMUL9dEgmepKYoeKhjZR-QLifRCWViazkJlKk (accessed 15 November 2019).

21 This section builds on comments made by Wolfgang Streeck in a seminar in LSE, London, 15 March 2019.

22 Matthew Karnitschnig, "Five Take-Aways from German CDU Chief's Vision for Europe," *Politico*, 3 October 2019, https://www.politico.eu/

article/5-takeaways-from-angela-merkel-proteges-annegret-kramp-karrenbauer-cdu-leader-vision-for-europe/ (accessed 15 November 2019).

23 Philip Oltermann and John Henley, "Germany's CDU leader denies rift with France over vision for Europe," *Guardian*, 11 March 2019, https://www.theguardian.com/world/2019/mar/11/germanys-cdu-leader-denies-rift-with-france-over-vision-for-europe (accessed 8 June 2019). On the redundancy of aircraft carriers, see "Aircraft carriers are big, expensive, vulnerable – and popular," *Economist*, 14 November 2019, https://www.economist.com/briefing/2019/11/14/aircraft-carriers-are-big-expensive-vulnerable-and-popular (accessed 19 November 2019).

24 See Wolfgang Münchau, "We Have Reached the End of the Franco-German Love-in," *Financial Times*, 14 April 2019.

25 "Emmanuel Macron in His Own Words," *Economist*, 7 November 2019, https://www.economist.com/europe/2019/11/07/emmanuel-macron-in-his-own-words-english (accessed 18 November 2019).

26 Wolfgang Münchau, "Changing the German Growth Model Will Not Be Easy," *Financial Times*, 13 May 2019.

27 I owe this point to Lee Jones. See further Paul Steinhardt, "The German Model," *The Full Brexit*, https://www.thefullbrexit.com/german-model (accessed 18 November 2019).

28 This specific figure is claimed by Wolfgang Streeck.

29 See in particular Lapavitsas, *Left Case*, and Martin Wolf, "How the Euro Helped Germany Avoid Becoming Like Japan," *Financial Times*, 29 October 2019.

30 Münchau, "Changing the German Growth Model."

31 See also Ambrose Evans Pritchard, "Italy's Salvini Throws in the Towel on Euro-Scepticism, Following the Lead of France's Le Pen," *Daily Telegraph*, 16 October 2019.

32 For a useful review of some of these, see Ambrose Evans-Pritchard, "The Euro Has Failed, Threatens Democracy, and Should Be Abolished," *Daily Telegraph*, 2 January 2019.

33 This point in particular was stressed by Streeck (fn. 12 above).

34 Roger Cohen, "Crisis in the Balkans, Germany's Mood: In a Breach, Germany Party Backs 'Limited Halt' in Kosovo Air War," *New York Times*, 14 May 1999, www.nytimes.com/1999/05/14/world/crisis-balkans-germany-s-mood-breach-german-party-backs-limited-halt-kosovo-air.html (accessed 7 March 2019).

35 For examples of this, see for instance, Alex Colas, "The Internationalist Disposition," *The Disorder of Things*, 4 January 2019, thedisorderofthings.com/tag/alex-colas/ (accessed 7 March 2019); Lea Ypi, "There is No Left Wing Case for Brexit: 21st-century Socialism Requires Transnational Organization," *LSE British Politics and Policy blog*, 22 November 2018, http://blogs.lse.ac.uk/politicsandpolicy/no-left-wing-case-for-brexit/

(accessed 7 March 2019); and Peter Verovšek, "Lexit Undermines the Left – It Will Be No Prize for Labour," 16 October 2018, https://blogs.lse.ac.uk/brexit/2018/10/16/lexit-undermines-the-left-it-will-be-no-prize-for-labour/ (accessed 19 June 2019).

36 Mark Mazower, *No Enchanted Palace: The End of Empire and the Ideological Origins of the United Nations* (Princeton: Princeton University Press, 2009), 18 and passim.

37 Carr, *Twenty Years' Crisis*, 148.

38 See also Guy Chazan, "World's Biggest Inland Port Puts German Rustbelt on China's Map," *Financial Times*, 8 April 2019.

39 This is a point made by James Heartfield, "European Union: A Process without a Subject," in *Politics without Sovereignty: A Critique of Contemporary International Relations*, ed. Christopher J. Bickerton, Philip Cunliffe, and Alex Gourevitch (London: UCL Press, 2007).

40 See, e.g., Andrew Linklater, "E.H. Carr, Nationalism and the Future of the Sovereign State," in *E.H. Carr: A Critical Appraisal*, ed. Michael Cox (Basingstoke: Palgrave, 2000) and William E. Scheuerman, *The Realist Case for Global Reform* (Cambridge: Polity, 2011), esp. chs. 2–3; see also Ken Booth, "Security in Anarchy: Utopian Realism in Theory and Practice," *International Affairs* 67, no. 3 (1991): 527–45.

41 Linklater, "Nationalism and the Future of the Sovereign State." Furthermore, as we have already seen, Robert Cox himself drew on Carr for his own historically informed accounts of change in international order (see ch. 2).

42 E.H. Carr, *Nationalism and After* (London: Macmillan, 1945), 36.

43 Carr, *Conditions of Peace* (London: Macmillan, 1942), 254.

44 Carr, *Nationalism and After*, 64–5.

45 E.g., see Erich Fromm, *The Fear of Freedom* (Abingdon: Routledge, 2001), passim; Max Horkheimer, "The Authoritarian State," *Telos* 15 (1973): 3–20.

46 Jonathan Haslam, *The Vices of Integrity: E.H. Carr 1892–1982* (London: Verso, 1999), 59.

47 Linklater, "Nationalism and the Future of the Sovereign State," 248, and 246–8; see also Haro L. Karkour, "Debating Global Justice with Carr: The Crisis of Laissez Faire and the Legitimacy Problem in the Twenty-first Century," *Journal of International Political Theory* (2019): doi: 1755088219838295.

48 Carr, *Conditions of Peace*, 8–10.

49 Kenealy and Kostagiannis are among the few "critical Carrians" that do acknowledge this; see their "Realist visions of European Union," 234.

50 British politician Boris Johnson was pilloried by Eutopians in the British press for making this entirely coherent and eminently Carrian point. See Boris Johnson, "The EU Wants a Super-State, just as Hitler did," *Daily Telegraph*, 15 May 2016.

51 Carr, *Nationalism and After*, 35.

52 Ibid.

53 Ibid.

54 In addition to Carr, the argument in this section draws on Mark Mazower, *Dark Continent: Europe's Twentieth Century* (London: Penguin, 1998) and James Heartfield, *Unpatriotic History of the Second World War* (London: Zero Books, 2012).

55 Mazower, *Dark Continent*, 160; see also Carr, *Conditions of Peace*, 241–3.

56 This is one of the core arguments of Heartfield, *Unpatriotic History*.

57 Doubtless the British elite would have debased themselves before the Nazis just as much as their continental counterparts, and British industrialists would have been happy to have had foreign storm-troopers to resolve industrial relations for them. They were deprived of this opportunity, not through their inner élan or national fortitude, but because the Germans didn't have radar and because even without British control of the air, the Royal Navy would have been able to sink any German invasion fleet. See RUSI, "The Battle of Britain Debate," 20 October 2006, https://rusi.org/commentary/battle-britain-debate (accessed 7 March 2019).

58 See also David Edgerton, *The Rise and Fall of the British Nation: A Twentieth Century History* (Penguin, 2019), 66.

59 See especially *The Twilight of Comintern 1930–1935* (London: Macmillan, 1982), esp. ch. 18. The work of Keith Smith is one of the exceptions in that he engages directly with Carr's studies of Soviet foreign policy and relates this to Carr's realism; see Keith Smith, "The Realism that Did Not Speak its Name: E.H. Carr's Diplomatic Histories of the Twenty Years' Crisis," *Review of International Studies* 43, no. 3 (2017): 475–93. See also E.H. Carr, "The Third International," in Carr, *From Napoleon to Stalin and Other Essays* (London: Macmillan, 1980) and Carr, *The Comintern and the Spanish Civil War*, ed. Tamara Deutscher (New York: Pantheon Books, 1984).

60 See E.H. Carr, *The Soviet Impact on the Western World* (London: Macmillan, 1947), 71–3.

61 Carr himself was alert to the odd congruence between Wilsonianism and Stalinism – but never pursued this insight systematically. See Carr, *Soviet Impact*, 2–3.

62 Carr, *Conditions of Peace*, 259.

63 See, e.g., Carr, *International Relations*.

64 Carr, *Twenty Years' Crisis*, 3.

65 Ibid., 4.

66 On the "counter-revolution" in war, see Gabriel Kolko, *Century of War: Politics, Conflict and Society since 1914* (New York: New Press, 1995), passim, and Azar Gat, *A History of Military Thought: From the Enlightenment to the Cold War* (Oxford: Oxford University Press, 2001), Book III, Part II, "Conclusion."

67 The counter-revolution in diplomacy could probably be dated earlier, to the institutions of the UN, which were self-consciously designed to avoid

the democratic decentralization of the League by concentrating power in the hands of the five permanent members of the Security Council. See F.H. Hinsley, *Power and the Pursuit of Peace: Theory and Practice in the History of Relations between States* (Cambridge: Cambridge University Press, 1963), esp. chs. 14–16.

68 G.R. Berridge, *The Counter Revolution in Diplomacy and other essays* (Basingstoke, Palgrave, 2011), 14.

69 Ibid.

70 See, e.g., Peter Mair, *Ruling the Void: The Hollowing of Western Democracy* (London: Verso, 2013); Colin Hay, *Why We Hate Politics* (Cambridge: Polity, 2007).

71 Yannis Varoufakis, *Adults in the Room: My Battle with Europe's Deep Establishment* (London: Vintage, 2018).

72 The following section draws on Heartfield, "European Union," and Christopher J. Bickerton, *European Integration: From Nation-States to Member States* (Oxford: Oxford University Press, 2012).

73 Christopher Bickerton, "Member States in European Integration," n.d., unpublished draft, 3–4.

74 See Christopher Bickerton, "Nation-State to Member State: Trajectories of State Reconfiguration and Recomposition in Europe," n.d., unpublished draft. For a general overview of EU secrecy, see also Varoufakis, *Adults in the Room*, passim.

75 Vivian Schmidt cited in Bickerton, "Member States in European Integration," 11.

76 See also Richard Tuck, "The Left Case for Brexit," *Dissent*, 6 June 2016.

77 I owe this point to Daniel Matthews Ferrero.

78 Perry Anderson, *The New Old World* (London: Verso Books, 2009), esp. chs. 3 and 10, and passim.

79 Carr, *Nationalism and After*, 18.

80 Carr, *Conditions of Peace,* 275.

81 Simon Hix, "Choose Freedom: 28 Countries, 500mn People, and One of the Most Successful Liberalising Projects in History," 11 June 2016, blogs.lse.ac.uk/brexit/2016/06/10/choose-freedom-28-countries-500m-people-and-one-of-the-most-successful-liberalising-projects-in-history/ (accessed 8 March 2019).

82 Nicolaïdis and Howse, "My EUtopia …," 781.

83 Ibid.

84 In Carr's words, "all popular post-war theories of international politics are reflections, seen in an American mirror, of nineteenth-century liberal thought." Carr, *Twenty Years' Crisis*, 29.

85 Carr, cited in Brian Porter, "E.H. Carr – the Aberystwyth Years, 1936–47," in *E.H. Carr*, ed. Michael Cox, 51.

86 Francis Fukuyama, "The End of History," *The National Interest* (Summer 1989), 3.

87 G.W.F. Hegel, *Philosophy of History* (1831), www.marxists.org/reference/archive/hegel/works/hi/introduction-lectures.htm#q (accessed 8 March 2019).

88 Ken Macleod, en.wikiquote.org/wiki/Ken_MacLeod (accessed 8 March 2019). Emphasis in original.

CONCLUSION

1 Michael Cox, introduction to *The Twenty Years' Crisis, 1919–1939: An Introduction to the Study of International Relations*, by E.H. Carr (Basingstoke: Palgrave, 2001), 54.

2 Seán Molloy, *The Hidden History of Realism: A Genealogy of Power Politics* (Basingstoke: Palgrave, 2006), 63.

3 See, e.g., Christopher Layne, *The Peace of Illusions: American Grand Strategy from 1940 to the Present* (Ithaca: Cornell University Press, 2007).

4 This was a point made at a roundtable, "Carr's Crisis and Ours: 1939/2019," British International Studies Association annual conference, London, 12–14 June 2019.

5 Karl Marx, *The Eighteenth Brumaire of Louis Napoleon* (1852, multiple editions), www.marxists.org/archive/marx/works/1852/18th-brumaire/index.htm (accessed 11 March 2019).

6 Ken Booth, *Theory of World Security* (Cambridge: Cambridge University Press, 2007), ch. 9.

7 Max Weber, *Political Writings*, ed. Peter Lassman, trans. Ronald Speirs (Cambridge: Cambridge University Press, 1994), 362.

8 I borrowed this designation from the late Nick Rennger.

9 See, e.g., Chantal Mouffe, *For a Left Populism* (London: Verso Books, 2018).

10 Carr, *Twenty Years' Crisis*, 62.

11 For a contrasting view on Carr's Machiavellianism, see Graham Evans, "E.H. Carr and International Relations," *British Journal of International Studies* 1, no. 2 (1975): 95.

12 Hegel of course borrowed this from Schelling.

13 See further Hans J. Morgenthau's critique of what he calls Carr's "utopianism of power": Hans J. Morgenthau, "The Political Science of E.H. Carr," Review of E.H. Carr, *The Twenty Years' Crisis, Conditions of Peace, Nationalism and After, The Soviet Impact on the Western World*, *World Politics* 1, no. 1 (1948): 127–34.

14 See James Burnham, *The Machiavellians: Defenders of Freedom* (Endeavour Media, 2019 [1943]), esp. Part II.

15 Morgenthau, "Political Science," 130.

16 I owe this framing of the problems identified by Carr to Randall Germain.

Index

Aberystwyth University, 13, 29

Abyssinia, 37

academics, British, 115

Adler, Emmanuel, 64, 68

Afghanistan, 123

Africa, 99

aircraft carriers, 95–6

al-Assad, Bashar, 43, 61

Albania, 32–3, 39–40, 98

alchemy, political, 68

Aleksandar I, King, 119

Aleppo, 43

American Civil War, 97

American leadership and power, 18

Anderson, Perry, 113–14

anthropocentric politics, 24

anti-fascism, 122

anti-Semitism, 37

appeasement, consequences of, 121

Aquinas, Thomas, 17

Arab Spring, 126

Ashley, Richard K., 71–2

Augustine, St, 17

Austro-Hungarian Empire, 33

authoritarianism, 39–40, 43, 67–8

Baccaro, Lucio, 94

balance of power, 35, 72

Baltic states, 93
Bannon, Steve, 85
Belgrade, bombing of Chinese
    embassy in, 48
"Belt and Road" project, 101
Benz, Karl, 96
Berridge, G.R., 109
Bickerton, Christopher J., 109–11
Bismarck, Otto von, 52
Blair, Tony, 48, 54
Bolsanaro, Jair, 43, 83
Booth, Ken, 19, 41–2, 122–3
Brazil, 43, 83
Brexit, 6–12, 21, 39, 42–3, 55, 61, 87,
    89–92, 95–100, 106, 112–16, 122,
    124
British Empire, 35, 100, 103
Burke, Anthony, 22–4
Bush, George W., 17, 34, 72, 119

Cameron, David, 9–10
Cammack, Paul, 26
Campbell, David, 16–17
canonical texts, 5
"CANZUK" countries, 38
Carr, E.H., 5–13, 21–8, 32–41, 44–58,
    61–5, 68, 73, 76, 86–7, 90–4, 100,
    103–8, 111–16, 119–20, 123, 126–7;
    Memorial Lecture (2004), 29
"Carr studies," 29–39
Catholicism, medieval, 73
censorship of the Internet, 122
Central Europe, 4, 105
Chakrabarty, Dipesh, 100
Chamberlain, Neville, 101
charismatic leaders, 4–5, 13
Chávez, Hugo, 84
China: economic development
    of, 4, 23–4, 37, 40, 85; political
    system, 39, 69; power of, 50, 67–8;
    relations with, 13, 70; trade with, 8
Claude, Inis L. Jr, 35
Clausewitz, Carl von, 81

climate change, 4, 25
Clinton, Hillary, 21, 24–5, 58, 61, 83
Cold War, 37–8, 57, 63–7, 74, 76,
    80–1, 88, 123; ending of, 17, 66
collective solidarity, 58–9
Collini, Stefan, 38
Comintern, 107
commodity fetishism, 80
Commonwealth, the, 38
Comprehensive Test Ban Treaty, 44
Congress of Vienna, 36
conscription, 32
constructivism, 6, 30–1, 62–73, 85,
    121, 124
Conte, Giuseppe, 96–7
contractarian political thought, 69
Corbyn, Jeremy, 12, 81
cosmopolitanism, 54–5
counter-hegemony, 80–4, 87
Cox, Michael, 41–2
Cox, Robert, 18, 64, 73–88
"creative destruction," 15
Crimea, 49
"crisis," use of the word, 41–2
critical theory of international
    relations, 5–8, 13, 16–17, 19, 22–31,
    46, 48, 61–3, 73–88, 91–3, 104–5,
    120–1, 124; disciplinary status of,
    25–6
Czechoslovakia, 33, 105

Davies, Lord David, 13, 48, 93
decolonisation, 36
democracy, 39
democratic peace, theory of, 22, 36
democratisation, 12, 43
Derrida, Jacques, 16
Deutsch, Karl, 65
dictatorship, arguments for, 15
different worlds, 40
"disaster utopianism," 24
Disraeli, Benjamin, 52
Doha round of trade negotiations, 46

Duisburg, 101
Dunne, Tim, 21, 41–2
Dutch Revolt, 35

Eastern Europe, 4, 104–05
ecological damage, 4, 22
economics, 12
The Economist, 43
egotism, 70–1
Egypt, 40, 123
Eich, Stefan, 125
Eighty Years War (1568–1648), 35
el-Sisi, Abdel Fattah, 123
"end of history" thesis, 90, 116
English School of international
  politics, 69
English-speaking peoples, 26, 38
Enloe, Cynthia, 20
entrepreneurs, 67
Erdoğan, Recep, 43, 126
Ethiopia, 40
ethnic cleansing, 49
Eurocentrism, 91–2, 117
"Eurocracy," 111
euro currency, 46, 92–5
Europe, decline of, 100–01
European Central Bank, 96–7
European Coal and Steel
  Community, 103
European Commission, 102, 112–13
European Council, 109, 111
European Court of Justice (ECJ),
  102, 112, 116
European integration and European
  unity, 31, 45, 105–8
European International Studies
  Association convention (Barcelona,
  2017), 27
*European Journal of International
  Relations*, 21
European Parliament, 46, 102, 112
European Single Market and
  Customs Union, 102

European Union (EU), 3–4, 7–8,
  15, 31, 38, 45, 53, 58, 61, 81,
  89–90, 97–103, 110–17, 122, 124;
  permanent representatives at, 111;
  shortcomings of, 90, 102–3, 111,
  115, 117
Euroscepticism, 90, 96
Eurotrack poll, 90
Eurozone policy, 4–5, 38, 46, 55, 58,
  61, 92–7, 102, 113–17, 123–4
Eutopianism, 31, 47, 91–103, 107–9,
  113–16, 123; definition of, 91;
  financing of, 93–103

fascism, 32, 106, 121–2
federalism, 97, 104, 110
First World War, 7, 14, 33, 41, 108
Fischer, Joschka, 99
Fisher, Mark, 82–3
France, 8, 12, 40, 43, 46, 66, 95–9,
  105, 114, 116, 123
Franco, Francisco, 32
Frankfurt School, 104
Fraser, Nancy, 8
Fukuyama, Francis, 90–1, 116

Gaddafi, Muammar, 43
Gaddis, John L., 11
Gbagbo, Laurent, 43, 47
geopolitics, 3, 9, 23–5, 45, 123
Georgia, 122
Germany, 12, 37, 40, 44, 51–6, 70–1,
  95–7, 102
gilets jaunes, 8, 116, 122, 126
"Global Britain," 99
global financial crisis (2008), 11–12,
  42, 95, 115–16
globalisation, 3, 18–21, 25–6, 46, 77,
  82, 85–6, 91, 115–16, 122–5
gold standard, 94
"good neighbour" policy, 52
Goodwin, Matthew, 12
Gorbachev, Mikhail, 11, 66

"government by diplomacy," 109
Graeber, David, 81
Gramsci, Antonio, 75, 78–82, 85
Great Depression, 118
Greece, 46, 93, 115–16, 123–4
Grossraum, 36
Group of Eight (G8), 109, 115
Grove, Jairus Victor, 24

Haiti, 83
Hamilton, Alexander, 97
Hansen, Lene, 21
Hardt, Michael, 17, 81, 83
"harmony of interests" doctrine, 7,
    30–1, 53, 70
Harrington, Cameron, 22, 24
Hayek, F.A. von, 92–5
Heartfield, James, 70, 109
Hegel, G.W.F., 116–17, 47, 126
hegemony, 81–5; liberal, 8,
    15, 20, 26–30, 61. *See also*
    counter-hegemony
historicism, 126
Hitler, Adolf, 33, 105
Hix, Stephen, 115
Hobbes, Thomas, 69
Hobsbawm, Eric, 41
Hobson, John M., 91
Holloway, John, 81
"hollowing-out" of state institutions,
    31, 112–13
Hong Kong, 126
Hont, István, 42
Howse, Robert, 91, 115–16
humanitarian intervention, 37, 43,
    47–50, 54
human rights, 15–16, 47–50, 54, 99,
    125
Human Terrain System, 16
Hume, David, 35
Hungary, 58
Hussein, Saddam, 13, 43

idealism, 29, 35, 55, 57, 62; liberal, 121
Ikenberry, G.J., 33
"imperial internationalism"
    (Mazower), 100
India, 24, 37, 47, 50, 69
industrialisation, 8
intergovernmentalism, 112–13
International Criminal Court (ICC),
    47
internationalism, liberal, 9, 32–5,
    50, 55–6, 62; as the doctrine of
    permanent war, 56; ending of the
    era of, 4
international law, 48, 52–3, 57, 119
International Monetary Fund (IMF),
    82, 115
international order, 4, 7, 14, 50, 55–8,
    67–72; viewed as a social construct,
    63, 72. *See also* liberal international
    order
international relations as a formal
    discipline: criticisms made of, 26;
    expansion of, 19–22; ideological
    commitment to warfare, 15;
    problems for, 3, 5
international society, 68–71; types
    of, 67
International Studies Association
    congress (Atlanta, 2016), 20–1
Iran, 39, 43, 67–8, 72
Iraq, 42, 49, 72, 119, 122–3
Iraq War (1990–91), 13
Iraq War (2003), 13–14
Ireland, 83
Islamic State, 15
Islamism, 78
Italy, 12, 33, 39–40, 44, 51, 58, 80–3,
    94, 115, 123

Jahn, Beate, 33, 64
Japan, 44, 51, 70
Jefferson, Thomas, 97
"just war" thinking, 17

Kant, Immanuel, 34, 69
Kantian society, 67
Kauṭilya, 126
Kellog-Briand Pact (1928), 53
Kennan, George F., 11
Kissinger, Henry, 48
Kojève, Alexandre, 18
Kosovo War (2009), 46–50, 53
Kramp-Karrenbaue, Annegret, 95–6

Labour Party, British, 12, 81
Lagarde, Christine, 96–7
Lake, David, 21–2
League of Nations, 8, 14, 34–5, 53, 56, 59, 93–4, 103–4, 108, 121
Lebow, Richard Ned, 67–71
left populism, 46
Lenin, V.I., 52, 78–9, 107
liberal international order, 4, 9–14, 28–9, 36, 42–3, 51, 54, 58–62, 121–2
liberalism in international relations, 34–7, 55–60; contemporary, 8–9; hostility to, 10–11
Libya, 40, 88, 99
Lighthizer, Robert, 85
Linklater, Andrew, 104
Locke, John, 69
Lockean society, 67
Louis Napoleon, 123
Lugard, Lord, 37
"Lula" da Silva, Luiz Ignácio, 83

Machiavelli, Niccolò, 78–9, 126–7
MacLeod, Ken, 117
Macron, Emmanuel, 8, 10, 55, 61, 89, 95–9, 114, 122; "Letter to Europe," 89, 95
Maduro, Nicolás, 86
mandate system, 52
Marinković, Vojislav, 119
Marx, Karl, 79–80, 123
mass politics and mass democracy, 31, 109

Mazower, Mark, 100
McQueen, Alison, 121
Mearsheimer, John J., 15, 29–30, 61
member-state theory, 109–14
mid-range theory, 21–2
Millennium (journal), 20, 24
Milošević, Slobodan, 43, 99
Mises, Ludwig von, 92–3
Mittel-Europe, 37
Morgenthau, Hans J., 28, 35
Moyn, Samuel, 10, 115
Münchau, Wolfgang, 96
Mussolini, Benito, 32–3

naive observations, 40–1
Napoleon, 123
nationalism, 4, 105; in the Third World, 17
nation-building, 16–17, 52
nation-states, 15, 23–4, 81, 106, 109, 126
nationhood, 106
Negri, Antonio, 17, 81
neo-conservatives, 54, 122, 123-4
neoliberalism, 8, 18, 67, 85, 123
Netherlands, the, 102
New International Economic Order, 76, 84
Nicolaïdis, Kalypso, 91, 115–16
Nicolson, Harold, 109
"9/11" attacks, 44
Non-Aligned Movement, 76
Noriega, Manuel, 43
North American Free Trade Agreement (NAFTA), 8, 58
North Atlantic Treaty Organisation (NATO), 16–17, 45–9, 53–4, 65–6, 77, 88, 97, 99
North Korea, 27, 43, 71, 88
nuclear weapons and nuclear deterrence, 42, 44, 88

Obama, Barack, 44

oil prices, 45, 53
"organic intellectuals," 81–2
"organising tendency" (Claude), 35–6
Oskanian, Kevork, 45

Palestine, 40
Panama, 53
paradigm wars, 66, 74
Paris climate agreement (2015), 43
Paris peace settlement (1919), 4, 51, 56–7
peacebuilding operations, 17, 37
peacekeeping operations, 8, 16, 56–7, 102
peace treaties, 4–5, 50–1
Pearl Harbour, 65
planetary politics, 22–4
Podemos, 125
populism, 13, 46, 84, 125
Porter, Brian, 48
post-Fordism, 78–86
post-political era, 124
"Pottery Barn" rule, 24
Powell, Colin, 24
power structures, 7, 21, 28, 36. *See also* balance of power
problem-solving theory, 74–5, 78
"progressive" neoliberalism, 8
propaganda, 54
protest movements, 43
public opinion, 51–5
Putin, Vladimir, 11, 44–5, 61, 96, 98, 122

Reagan, Ronald, 84
realism regarding international relations, 14, 27–30, 34, 58, 92, 103–4, 120, 125–7. *See also* structural realism
reflexivity, 73–4
refugees, 37
regime change, 43, 67

regulatory monitoring, 112
Renzi, Matteo, 12
Richelieu, Cardinal, 109
Rorty, Richard, 13
Rove, Karl, 72
Rubin, James, 17
rules-based order, 50
Russia: democratisation in, 69; geopolitical relations with, 13, 54, 69–70, 96, 115, 124; military power and proxy warfare, 3, 49–53, 67–8, 98–9; political system and leadership, 11, 39, 44–5, 52, 106–7
Russian Revolution, 41

Saudi Arabia, 39, 67–8
Schmidt, Vivian, 112
Schmittianism, 125
scientific thought, 7
Second World War 33, 105
"security communities," 65–6
Seven Years' War (1756–63), 35
Singapore, 65
Sino-Japanese War, 101
Slobodian, Quinn, 92
Smith, Keith, 29
Smuts, Jan, 100
socialisation, 70
South Africa, 67–8
sovereignty, 48–54, 57–8, 72; pooling of, 113
Soviet Union: disintegration of, 17, 42. *See also* Russia
Spain, 46, 98
Spanish Civil War, 32
Speer, Albert, 106
Spivak, Gayatri, 22–3
Stability and Growth Pact, 114
Stalin, Joseph, 107
status quo powers, 8, 50–3, 73
structural realism, 66–7, 74–5
sub-national units, 98
summitry, 109

Sun Tzu, 81
supranationalism, 58, 103, 126
Syria, 37, 43, 122–3
Syriza, 81, 125

terrorism, 42
Thatcher, Margaret, 84
Thirty Years' War (1618–48), 41
threats of force, 52
Tooze, Adam, 41, 95, 125
totalitarian regimes, 9, 11
trade negotiations, 46
trade wars, 3
triceratops, 11
Trump, Donald, 4, 6, 10, 12, 15, 21,
    24, 27, 37, 41–4, 61, 82–8, 104, 119
trusteeship, 49
Tuck, Richard, 112
Turkey, 39, 43, 67–8, 110
"turns" in theorising, 61

Ukraine, 45, 99–101, 122
unipolarity, 17–25; definition of, 28
United Kingdom: academia in, 115;
    decision to leave the European
    Union, see Brexit; party system in,
    12, 46; power of, 8, 38, 51, 56, 100.
    See also British Empire; "Global
    Britain"
United Nations, 35, 37, 56, 59, 77,
    103, 107, 124; Charter, 50; sanctions
    against Iraq, 13; Security Council,
    13, 17, 34, 36, 47–50, 53
United States, 3, 8, 13–14, 46, 56, 58,
    70–3, 97–8, 116–17; military spend-
    ing, 44; Supreme Court, 96, 112
Uruguay round of trade negotiations,
    46
utopianism, 5–11, 21, 24–31, 36,
    39, 44–5, 49–53, 57, 61–79,

90–7, 101, 103, 111, 119–21,
    124–5; characteristics of, 6–8;
    construction of novel forms
    of, 64–73; critical, 25–31, 73–8;
    definition of, 91

Varoufakis, Yannis, 110–11
Venezuela, 15
Vico, Giambattista, 75–6
Volkswagen scandal (2015), 96

Walt, Stephen M., 15, 30, 61
Waltz, Kenneth, 88, 75
Walzer, Michael, 14–15
war on terror, 13, 42
weapons of mass destruction, 13
Weber, Cynthia, 25
Weber, Max, 125–6
Wendt, Alexander, 64–8, 71, 87–8
Westphalian: powers, 50, 78; treaties,
    24
Whitworth, Sandra, 16
Wight, Colin, 21
Williams, Gavin, 40
Wilson, Woodrow, 8, 13, 34–5, 41,
    51–2, 56–7, 108
Wiskemann, Elizabeth, 41
Woolf, Leonard, 100
World Social Forum, 83
World Trade Organisation (WTO),
    58, 91, 115–16; protests at Seattle
    meeting of (1999), 45–6, 82

Yanukovych, Viktor, 43
Yeltsin, Boris, 44–5
Yugoslavia, 47–8, 105

Žižek, Slavoj, 10, 125